# A Statement of Faith

*Minister.*

**Let** us repeat together a contemporary expression of Christian faith.*

*Minister and People.*

We believe in God, the eternal Spirit,
   Father of our Lord Jesus Christ and our Father,
   and to his deeds we testify:
He calls the worlds into being,
   creates man in his own image
   and sets before him the ways of life and death.
He seeks in holy love to save all people from aimlessness and sin.
He judges men and nations by his righteous will
   declared through prophets and apostles.

In Jesus Christ, the man of Nazareth, our crucified and risen Lord,
   he has come to us
   and shared our common lot,
   conquering sin and death
   and reconciling the world to himself.

He bestows upon us his Holy Spirit,
   creating and renewing the church of Jesus Christ,
   binding in covenant faithful people
   of all ages, tongues and races.

He calls us into his church
   to accept the cost and joy of discipleship,
   to be his servants in the service of men,
   to proclaim the gospel to all the world
     and resist the powers of evil,
   to share in Christ's baptism and eat at his table,
   to join him in his passion and victory.

He promises to all who trust him
   forgiveness of sins and fullness of grace
   courage in the struggle for justice and peace,
   his presence in trial and rejoicing,
   and eternal life in his kingdom which has no end.

**Blessing** and honour, glory and power be unto him. *Amen.*

*Statement of Faith of the United Church of Christ in the U.S.A.

# SERVICE BOOK

*for*
*the use of ministers*
*conducting*
*public worship*

*Published for*
**THE UNITED CHURCH OF CANADA**
*by*
**THE RYERSON PRESS**

**1969**

©THE RYERSON PRESS, 1969
SBN 7700 0281 1

PRINTED AND BOUND IN CANADA
BY THE RYERSON PRESS, TORONTO

# Preface

Following union in 1925, General Council set up a Committee on Church Worship to prepare a Book of Common Order for The United Church of Canada. The new book prepared by the Committee was accepted by General Council in 1932 and authorized for use in the Church.

In 1958 General Council instructed the Committee on Worship to revise the Book of Common Order (1932). The Committee, with permission, has divided the Book of Common Order into three Service Books. This book, the Service Book for the use of ministers conducting public worship, is the first of the three. The second, the Service Book for the use of the people, is also now being published. The third, the Service Book for use in Church Courts, is in preparation but will not be available for some time. General Council in 1968 authorized the first two for use in the Church.

As our forefathers did in 1932, "the Committee prays that those who use this book may be enabled to enter more fully into the rich heritage of Christian Worship" and be stimulated to explore, under the guidance of the Holy Spirit, new ways of worship.

Glory be to God.

Lent 1969

# ACKNOWLEDGMENTS

The editors and publisher have made every effort to trace the ownership of all copyrighted material and to secure permission from holders of such rights. If any question arises as to the use of any material the publisher and editors, while expressing regret for any inadvertent error, will be pleased to make the necessary corrections in future printings. Thanks are due to the following authors, publishers, publications and agents for permission to use selections from the material indicated.

Abingdon Press: *Prayers for Christian Services*, Carl A. Glover, 1959.

British Broadcasting Corporation: *New Every Morning*, 1955.

Cambridge University Press: *New English Bible; The Book of Common Worship of the Church of South India*.

Collins Fontana: *The Plain Man's Book of Prayers*, William Barkley, 1959.

Episcopal Diocese of Massachusetts, Church Service League: *Prayers for the Church Service League*, 1937.

Forward Movement Press: *Prayers New and Old*.

Harper and Row, Publishers: *Prayers of the Spirit*, John W. Suter; *A Book of Public Prayer*.

Independent Press: *Prayers and Services for Christian Festivals*, James M. Todd, 1959.

Indian Society for Promoting Christian Knowledge: *A Book of Common Prayer (1960) of the Church of India, Pakistan, Burma and Ceylon*.

Longmans Green and Company Limited: *A Cambridge Bede Book*, E. M. White; *Per Chrustum Vinces*, Barton.

Macmillan Company of Canada Limited: *Handbook of Public Prayer*, Roger Geffen, 1963.

National Council of Churches of Christ in the U.S.A.: The Scripture quotations in this publication are from the *Revised Standard Version Bible*, copyright 1946 and 1952 by the Division of Christian Education, National Council of the Churches of Christ in the U.S.A. and used by permission.

Oxford University Press: *The Book of Common Order of the Anglican Church of Canada*, 1955; *The Book of Common Order, Church of Scotland*, 1940, by permission of the Committee on Public Worship and Aids to Devotion of the Church of Scotland; *The Book of Common Prayer* is Crown copyright and extracts are used by permission; *The Book of Common Worship of the Church of South India* by permission of the Synod of the Church of South India; *A Book of Public Worship* compiled for the use of Congregationalists, Huxtable, Marsh, Micklem and Todd, 1948; *Daily Prayer*, ed. Eric Milner-White and G. W. Briggs, 1959; *Diary of Private Prayers*, John Baillie, 1936; *Let Us Pray*, by permission of the Committee on Public Worship and Aids to Devotion of the Church of Scotland and Oxford University Press; *New English Bible; Prayers for the Christian Year*, (revised edition) by permission of the Committee on Public Worship and Aids to Devotion of the Church of Scotland; *Westminster Prayers*, ed. P. Dearmer and F. R. Barry.

Pilgrim Press: *Church Worship Book*, Charles W. Merriam, 1931.

Society for Promoting Christian Knowledge, Holy Trinity Church, London: *The Splendour of God*, Anglican Evangelical Movement, 1961; *A Manual of Eastern Orthodox Prayers; A War Primer*.

Student Christian Movement Press: *Contemporary Prayers for Public Worship*, ed. Carlye Micklem, 1967, by permission of S.C.M. Press; *A Devotional Diary; Pilgrimage to Amsterdam*, Canon H. G. G. Herklots, 1948.

Westminster Press: *The Book of Common Worship*, Provisional Services. The Westminster Press. Copyright © 1966, W. L. Jenkins. Used by permission.

World Student Christian Federation: *Venite Adoremus*, English translation of the High Mass of the Church of Sweden.

# INTRODUCTION

The services in this book are for the guidance and assistance of those leading or sharing in public worship. They are not provided to enforce compliance or uniformity.

In the United Church of Canada there are no prescribed forms of worship, except part of the ordination service. Worship in the United Church of Canada is guided by directories. This means that liberty is given to each minister to use his own words in any prayer. In a directory rubrics refer to structure and content, not language. It is in this context that the use of "shall" and "may" in the rubrics is to be understood. "Shall" indicates not prescription but preference, a recommendation that an act should be done or a type of prayer said. "May" suggests some particular act or prayer but without the preference involved in "shall".

The prayers and scripture readings in the various services and in Section II, Material for Services of Worship, are samples of what may be appropriately used in public worship. Freedom is given to any minister to adapt them to local circumstances or to provide his own.

\*　　　\*　　　\*

Three general concerns underlie the services in this book and have helped to shape them. These concerns are not peculiar to the United Church of Canada but are characteristic of liturgical revision in other churches.

## Unity of Word and Sacrament

One concern is to emphasize the unity of word and sacrament. Implicit here is acceptance of the sacrament of the Lord's supper as the basic Christian service and as such normative for Christian worship. No indication is given as to how often the sacrament of the Lord's supper should be celebrated, although it is acknowledged that the early church did so weekly. It should be observed, however, that the first order for public worship is based on the pattern of the Lord's supper. This is also the shape of the orders for confirmation, marriage and, to some extent, burial.

The emphasis on the unity of word and sacrament has also meant that the sacrament of baptism is given as a complete order rather than an insert in an abbreviated order for Sunday worship. Baptism is administered after the word has been read and proclaimed.

## Worship as Action

Another concern is to emphasize action as characteristic of worship. Worship is something which is done; Christian worship is something which Christians do. Primarily, of course, it is God's action. The chief agent in worship is God who speaks and acts in word and sacrament. It is his word which comes in scripture and sermon and which is made manifest in the sacraments of baptism and the Lord's supper. To his word we respond. Our response should not be thought of only in terms of listening or watching. It involves action.

To bring out the element of action the services have been composed with a simple, ongoing movement. An effort has been made to avoid repetition or ornamentation. This is seen, for example, in the sacrament of the Lord's supper, where the action involved in the four verbs "take", "bless", "break", "give", which goes back to Christ's action in the Upper Room, is brought out clearly. Nothing interrupts this direct, developing movement. Provision is also made in this service for particular actions by the congregation such as the presenting of the bread and wine at the offertory, and the giving of the peace with appropriate gestures.

There is also an effort in the services to relate worship to the action of the Christian in the world. One way in which this is done has been to conclude each service with a commissioning, a sending of the community of faith into the world. But there is also an acceptance of the fact that what Christians do in the world should affect what they do at worship. The prayers in the services and in the Material for Services of Worship have been selected because of their concreteness and relevance to particular situations.

## Worship as Social Action

The third concern is to emphasize the essentially corporate aspect of public worship. The word "liturgy" literally means people's work. This indicates that the celebrant at public worship is not the minister but the people. The minister presides over the people's worship and as president has certain parts which are peculiarly his. But the worship is not his alone. It belongs to the whole community of God's people.

The services have, therefore, been devised to provide as much participation by the people as possible, not only through the singing of hymns and the reading of psalms but also through the prayers. Some of the prayers are to be said in unison and in others the opportunity is given for congregational response. Both in the services and in the Material for Services of Worship there are examples of bidding prayers with opportunities for silent prayer by the people.

The people may participate in other ways. For example, members of the congregation may read the scripture lessons and lead in prayer. Opportunity should be provided for members to request special thanksgivings and intercessions so that the prayers reflect the vital concerns of the people.

To encourage and provide for congregational participation the United Church of Canada has prepared a *Service Book for the use of the people*. This people's book contains the basic services, a collection of prayers and an arrangement of the prose psalms.

Related to the subject of worship being truly congregational is the difficult issue of the nature of the language to be used. For the scripture passages the Revised Standard Version has been employed, although in some selections from the New Testament other modern translations have been used. For the prayers the aim has been to shun the generalities of many of the prayers of the past and to emphasize the particularity and concreteness characteristic of our age. The form of address to God varies. In the first order for the celebration of the Lord's supper, God is addressed as "thou". In the second he is addressed as "you", and the implications of this form of address have been worked out in sentence structure and imagery. In the Material for Services of Worship, examples of prayers in contemporary language have been provided.

\*     \*     \*

Many ministers and lay people have contributed to the *Service Book*. The first draft of each service was submitted to the presbyteries for consideration. In the light of the comments received each service was then revised and sent to ministers for experimental use in congregations. The final revision has taken account of what ministers, sessions and individual lay people had to say concerning the second draft. When the 23rd General Council authorized the use of this Service Book it gave the Worship Committee authority to prepare and issue additional contemporary services. As a result a second order for both Baptism and Adult Baptism and Confirmation have been added. It is hoped that the *Service Book* will assist the people in their worship of God to whom alone belongs the glory.

# Contents

# I. SERVICES OF WORSHIP

## 1. SERVICES FOR THE CELEBRATION OF THE LORD'S SUPPER

### Introduction

Word and sacrament make up the normal act of worship on the Lord's day. The combination of spoken word and "visible word" gives the complete pattern upon which orders for the celebration of the sacrament are founded.

The first two orders have a simple, direct structure. Following a brief Approach, the Word of God is read and preached. The intercessions are made after the sermon when minds have been kindled and sympathies stirred. The third part, the Word of God Enacted, follows without interruption the fourfold action of Christ in the Upper Room — he took (offertory), gave thanks (prayer of thanksgiving), broke (fraction) and gave (communion).

Both orders emphasize the element of thanksgiving. Stress is laid upon the resurrection and victory of Christ.

The second order is an attempt to express the thought and language of the first order in a colloquial idiom. In it a suggestion is made for the restoration of a visible act of mutual greeting, symbolizing unity in Christ. In the first order the greeting is expressed in dialogue between minister and people.

The third order is that which was in the *Book of Common Order* (1932 and 1950). Minor emendations in rubrics have been made to remove ambiguities and to suggest the better of alternatives.

The fourth order is a very simple form of celebration suitable for house or group occasions.

Communion may be received in a variety of ways. The people may remain in the pews, the elders carrying the bread and wine to them; the people may go forward and receive kneeling, or standing, at the chancel steps; or the people may gather in a group around the Table.

An order for the communion of the sick is not provided. In some cases, minister, elder and members of the family may participate in a shortened celebration in the sick room. In other cases it may be necessary for the service so to be curtailed that it consists only of the words of institution, prayer, distribution of the bread and wine, and a blessing.

AN OUTLINE FOR

## THE CELEBRATION OF

## THE LORD'S SUPPER

*The Approach*  Scripture Sentences
Prayer of Approach
Hymn
Confession of Sin
Assurance of Pardon
Doxology or Hymn

*The Word of*  Prayer for Grace
*God*  Old Testament
*Proclaimed*  Epistle
*and*  Psalm
*Acknowledged*  Gospel
Sermon
Prayer or Ascription
Creed or Te Deum
Hymn
Prayers of Intercession and Commemoration of the Dead
Banns and Announcements

*The Word*  Invitation
*of God*  Peace
*Enacted*  Offertory
Prayer of Thanksgiving and Consecration
Lord's Prayer
Fraction
Distribution
Prayers of Thanksgiving and Supplication
Hymn
Commissioning
Blessing

AN ORDER FOR
## THE CELEBRATION OF
## THE LORD'S SUPPER
based on the foregoing outline

### The Approach

*The people having assembled, the minister shall call them to worship with sentences from Holy Scripture appropriate to the season of the Christian Year concluding with the following,*

What shall I render to the Lord for all his bounty to me?

I will lift up the cup of salvation and call on the name of the Lord.                    *Psalm 116. 12, 13*

*A prayer of approach appropriate to the season of the Christian Year, or the following, shall be said,*

Almighty God, unto whom all hearts be open, all desires known, and from whom no secrets are hid: cleanse the thoughts of our hearts by the inspiration of thy Holy Spirit, that we may perfectly love thee, and worthily magnify thy holy name; through Christ our Lord. **Amen.**

*A hymn of praise shall be sung.*

*A prayer of general confession shall be said by minister and people.*

**O God, Father, Son and Holy Spirit,**
    **we confess to thee**
        **and to all the company of heaven**
        **and to one another**
    **that we have sinned**
        **in thought, word and deed,**
        **and by omission,**
    **through our fault, our own grievous fault.**

*Then the minister shall call the people to make their private confession of sin, saying,*

Let each of us in silence humbly confess his sins to almighty God.

*After a period of silence the following may be sung or said,*

**O Lamb of God, who takest away the sin of the world, have mercy upon us;**

**O Lamb of God, who takest away the sin of the world, have mercy upon us;**

**O Lamb of God, who takest away the sin of the world, grant us thy peace.**

*The minister shall give an assurance of pardon.*

Here are words you may trust, words that merit full acceptance.

Christ Jesus came into the world to save sinners. If we confess our sins, he is just, and may be trusted to forgive our sins and cleanse us from every kind of wrong.

Therefore in the name of the Father and of the Son and of the Holy Spirit, I assure you that God has forgiven you your sins.

*Then may be sung a doxology or a suitable hymn of praise.*

**The Word of God Proclaimed and Acknowledged**

*A prayer for grace appropriate to the season of the Christian Year shall be said.*

*A lesson from the Old Testament, or from a book of the New Testament other than a gospel, or from both, appropriate to the season of the Christian Year, shall be read.*

*A psalm or canticle shall be sung or said, with this conclusion, wherever appropriate,*

**Glory be to the Father,**
   **and to the Son,**
   **and to the Holy Spirit;**
**as it was in the beginning,**
   **is now, and ever shall be:**
      **world without end. Amen.**

*A lesson from one of the gospels appropriate to the season of the Christian Year shall be read.*

*A sermon shall be preached.*

*Prayer or an ascription shall follow.*

To him who loves us and freed us from our sins with his life's blood, who made of us a royal house, to serve as the priests of his God and Father — to him be glory and dominion for ever and ever! **Amen.**

*Then the minister and people may make profession of the faith of the church by singing or saying the Nicene Creed or the Apostles' Creed or We praise thee, O God.*

*A hymn may be sung.*

*Prayers of intercession and commemoration of the dead shall follow.*

*Minister.*

Let us pray for the peace of the whole world, for the extension of God's kingdom and for the salvation of all men. *Silence.* Lord, hear our prayer:

*People.*

**And in thy love answer.**

*Minister.*

Let us pray for the well-being of the churches of God and for the unity of them all, that they may fulfil their mission in the world. *Silence.* Lord, hear our prayer:

*People.*
**And in thy love answer.**

*Minister.*

Let us pray for ministers of word and sacrament, for missionaries, for elders and teachers, and for all who bear office in the church, that they may be faithful to the work committed to them. *Silence.* Lord, hear our prayer:

*People.*
**And in thy love answer.**

*Minister.*

Let us pray for all who profess the name of Christ, and for any who this day sit at the Table of the Lord for the first time, that they may be kept in the way of salvation. *Silence.* Lord, hear our prayer:

*People.*
**And in thy love answer.**

*Minister.*

Let us pray for all entrusted with authority in nation and community, that they may order all things with justice and mercy. *Silence.* Lord, hear our prayer:

*People.*

**And in thy love answer.**

*Minister.*

Let us pray for the lonely and the troubled, for the sick and the sorrowful, and for those to whom death draws near, that they may be comforted. *Silence.* Lord, hear our prayer:

*People.*

**And in thy love answer.**

*Minister.*

Let us pray for any whom we wish to remember by name. *Silence.* Lord, hear our prayer:

*People.*

**And in thy love answer.**

*Minister.*

Remembering what thy love has accomplished in thy saints, and thy faithfulness to those who have gone before us into thy presence, we commend ourselves and one another, and all our life, to Christ our Lord.

*People.*

**Help, save and strengthen us, O God, by thy grace. Amen.**

*Banns of marriage may be published and such announcements as are needful and fitting shall be made.*

**The Word of God Enacted**

*The minister may say,*

In the name of Jesus Christ I invite all who profess him as Lord and Saviour, and are seeking to follow in his way and to live in unity one with the other, to come to his Table with reverence, faith and thanksgiving. Eat and drink for your strengthening that you may grow in grace and be blessed with all spiritual blessings, remembering that we, although many, are one body in him.

*Minister.*

Peace be with you;

*People.*

**And love to one another.**

*Minister.*

Christ is in the midst of us:

*People.*

**He is, and he will be!**

*The offerings of the people shall be collected.*

*A hymn shall then be sung, such as* Ye gates, lift up your heads on high, *during which the offerings shall be presented, the people standing.*

*The bread and wine may be brought forward at the same time and placed on the Table.*

*And the bread and wine shall be uncovered.*

*An offertory prayer shall be said.*

Holy Father, who through the blood of thy dear Son hast consecrated for us a new and living way to thyself, we pray thee to accept and use us and these our gifts. All things come from thee and of thine own do we give thee; and to thee shall be the glory. **Amen.**

*The people may be seated.*

*The minister shall say, and the people shall answer, as follows,*

*Minister.*
Lift up your hearts;

*People.*
**We lift them up to the Lord.**

*Minister.*
Let us give thanks to him;

*People.*
**It is right so to do.**

*Minister.*
All glory and thanksgiving be to thee, almighty God, for creating the heavens and the earth and all that is in them, for making man in thine own image, and for watching mercifully over all that thou hast made.

*People.*
**Glory be to thee, O Lord.**

*Minister.*
All glory and thanksgiving be to thee, our heavenly Father, for redeeming us in Jesus Christ thine only Son, who took our nature upon him and in obedi-

ence accepted death, even death on a cross; who by thy power was raised from the dead and was exalted for evermore.

*People.*
**Glory be to thee, O Lord.**

*Minister.*
Therefore with all creation and with all the company of the redeemed we magnify thy glorious name, evermore praising thee, and saying,

*People.*
**Holy, holy, holy, Lord God of hosts,
    heaven and earth are full of thy glory.
Glory be to thee, O Lord most high.**

*Minister.*
Eternal God, King of heaven and earth:
the life and death of thy Son our Lord and Saviour
    Jesus Christ, we proclaim;
his resurrection from the dead and his ascension,
    we confess;
his coming in triumph, we await.

*People.*
**Even so, come Lord Jesus.**

*Minister.*
Wherefore, O Father, we set forth before thee this holy supper, following his command who the night in which he was betrayed took bread and blessed, and broke it, and gave it to his disciples, saying,

Take, eat: this is my body; who in the same way took the cup saying, This is my blood of the new covenant.

*People.*

**Worthy is the Lamb, the Lamb that was slain, to receive all power and wealth, wisdom and might, honour and glory and praise.**

*Minister.*

And now, Almighty God, we pray thee to send thy Holy Spirit that the bread which we break may be to us communion in the body of Christ, and the cup of blessing which we bless communion in the blood of Christ; that being built up in love we may be strengthened in the unity of the faith and come to the fulness of the stature of Christ.

*Minister and People.*

**And here, O Lord, in union with our Lord Christ, who gave himself for us and the world, and in fellowship with the whole church in heaven and on earth, we offer thee ourselves to be a living sacrifice, praying thee to accept us with this our worship of praise and thanksgiving.**
**This we ask trusting in the eternal sacrifice of Jesus Christ our Lord, by whom and with whom, in the unity of the Holy Spirit, all honour and glory be unto thee, O Father almighty, world without end. Amen.**

*Minister.*

And now, as our Saviour Christ has taught us, we say,

*Minister and people.*

**Our Father, who art in heaven,**
    **hallowed be thy name,**
    **thy kingdom come,**
    **thy will be done,**
    **on earth as it is in heaven.**
**Give us this day our daily bread,**
    **and forgive us our trespasses**
    **as we forgive those who trespass against us,**
    **and lead us not into temptation**
    **but deliver us from evil.**
**For thine is the kingdom, the power and the glory,**
    **for ever and ever. Amen.**

*Then the minister shall take the bread and breaking it shall say,*

The body of Christ broken for you.

*Then he shall take the cup and say,*

The blood of Christ shed for you.

*The minister shall receive the bread and wine. The elders and the people shall receive the bread and wine.*

*When the minister delivers the bread he shall say,*

The body of our Lord Jesus Christ keep you unto eternal life.

*When the minister delivers the cup he shall say,*

The blood of our Lord Jesus Christ keep you unto eternal life.

*What remains of the bread and wine shall be reverently placed upon the Table and covered.*

*A prayer of thanksgiving and supplication shall be said.*

Gracious God, we praise thee that in word and sacrament thou hast given us thy precious treasure, Jesus Christ the bread of life and the true vine; and we thank thee that thou hast brought us into communion with him and with one another; through Jesus Christ our Lord. **Amen.**

Grant, O Lord, that the ears which have heard the voice of thy songs may be closed to the voice of clamour and dispute; that the eyes which have seen thy great love may also behold thy blessed hope; that the tongues which have sung thy praise may speak the truth; that the feet which have walked thy courts may walk in the region of light; and that the bodies which have tasted thy living body may be restored to newness of life. Glory be to thee for thine inexpressible gift. **Amen.**

*A hymn shall be sung.*

*The minister shall commission the people.*

Go into the world in the power of the Holy Spirit to fulfil your high calling as servants and soldiers of Jesus Christ.

*And he shall dismiss them with a blessing.*

The peace of God, which passes all understanding, keep your hearts and minds in the knowledge and love of God, and of his Son Jesus Christ our Lord; and the blessing of God almighty, the Father, the Son and the Holy Spirit, be among you and remain with you always. **Amen.**

ANOTHER ORDER FOR
**THE CELEBRATION OF**
**THE LORD'S SUPPER**
based on the foregoing outline

## The Approach

*The service shall begin by the minister saying sentences from scripture appropriate to the season of the Christian Year. He shall conclude with,*

What shall I give to God for all he has given me?
I will thank him and acknowledge him before men.

*Psalm 116. 12, 17*

*A prayer of approach shall be said. It should be appropriate to the season of the Christian Year, but the following may be used,*

O God, how mighty you are.
You know all that is in us,
 all that we hope for,
 all that we try to hide.
Fill us with your Holy Spirit
 that our thoughts may be clean.
Help us to love you with all our being
 and to show by our actions
 that we are truly your people;
  through Christ our Lord. **Amen.**

*A hymn of praise shall be sung.*

*Minister and people shall say together a prayer of general confession.*

**We confess to you, God, that we have sinned**
 **in what we have thought, said and done.**
**We confess that we have sinned also**
 **in what we have not thought, or said, or done.**

**Before all your people we confess this to you,**
**we confess it openly to one another.**
**These our faults have hurt us and hurt others;**
**we cannot stand them any longer.**
**Help us.**
**Rid us of our guilt.**

*This shall be followed by a period of silence during which private confession shall be made.*

*At the close of the private confession there shall be said or sung,*

**Lord have mercy,**
**Christ have mercy,**
**Lord have mercy.**

*An assurance of pardon shall be given by the minister.*

Here is good news for you.

Christ Jesus came into the world to save sinners.

If we confess our sins, he is just, and may be trusted to forgive our sins and cleanse us from every kind of wrong.

So it is that I can assure you that your sins are forgiven.

*A doxology may follow.*

**The Word of God Proclaimed and Acknowledged**

*A prayer for grace shall be said. It should be appropriate to the season of the Christian Year.*

*A lesson shall be read. It will be from the Old Testament or the New Testament, but not the gospel, and will be appropriate to the season of the Christian Year. If desired two lessons may be read at this point, one from the Old Testament and the other from the New Testament.*

*A canticle or a psalm shall be sung or said. Where it is appropriate it will conclude with the following,*

**Glory be to the Father,**
   **and to the Son,**
   **and to the Holy Spirit;**
**as it was in the beginning,**
   **is now, and ever shall be:**
      **world without end. Amen.**

*A gospel lesson shall be read. It will be appropriate to the season of the Christian Year.*

*A sermon shall be preached.*

*At the close of the sermon there should be a prayer or an ascription.*

*A creed may be said.*

*A hymn may be sung.*

*Prayers of intercession of particular concern to the people shall be said. They should conclude with a remembrance of the dead.*

*Banns of marriage may be published and any necessary announcements made.*

## The Word of God Enacted

*Minister and people may declare their unity in Christ in this way:*

> *The minister and whoever is assisting him shall grasp each other either by the right hand or by the forearms. The minister shall say, "We are one in Christ," and the one addressed shall reply, "We are one indeed." Each shall then go to an elder, carry out the same action and say the same words. Thereupon the elders shall give the same greeting of action and word to one another and then to the first person in each pew. These persons shall then pass the greeting to the next person in the pew and so on until everyone in the congregation has expressed unity in Christ.*

*An offering shall be collected.*

*A hymn shall be sung during which the offering shall be brought forward.*

*At the same time the bread and wine shall be carried up to the Table and placed on it.*

*The bread and wine shall be uncovered.*

*An offertory prayer shall be said by minister and people.*

**We bring our gifts to you, O God.**
**Here is the labour of our hands.**
**Here is the love of our hearts.**
**Accept them and use them;**
**through Christ our Lord. Amen.**

*The people shall remain standing.*

*A prayer of thanksgiving and consecration shall be said.*

*Minister.*
Lift up your hearts;

*People.*
**We lift them up to the Lord.**

*Minister.*
Let us give thanks to him;

*People.*
**It is right to do so.**

*Minister.*
We thank you, God,
that you are mighty;
that you create everything,
this earth and the universe of which it is part;
that you make man like yourself and for yourself;
that you care for all that you make.

*People.*
**O God, how great you are.**

*Minister.*

We thank you, God,
that you give yourself;
you gave Jesus your son,
a man like us but unlike us faithful to you,
a man who died as we die but unlike us accepted
death even though it meant to be broken on a
cross.
We thank you
that you brought him to life again;
that he lives now;
that he will always live, exalted and triumphant.

*People.*

**O God, how good you are.**

*Minister.*

So it is that we, and all your people, are grateful
to you.
We acknowledge your greatness and goodness
by saying,

*People.*

**We thank you, God. We thank you.**
**Everything reveals how great and good you are.**
**We worship you.**

*Minister.*

Before you, God, by what we do here,
we celebrate the life and death of Jesus Christ;
we declare our faith that he is alive and master
of all;
we witness to the hope that he will come again.

*People.*

**Come, Lord Jesus, come.**

*Minister.*

So it is we do what Jesus did the night he was
  betrayed.
He took bread, thanked you, broke the bread and
  gave it to his followers, saying,
"Take, eat, this is my body."
He also took the cup, saying,
"This is my blood, the blood of the new covenant."

*People.*

**Worthy is Christ, Christ the sacrificed, to be
praised and served.**

*Minister.*

Send your Holy Spirit, God, on us and what we do
  that as we break bread and drink wine
  we may be united with Christ,
  he in us and we in him,
  that we who are many may be one in him.
Make us strong in faith and love
  that we may become true men
  as Christ was truly man.

*Minister and People.*

**As our Lord Jesus Christ offered himself to you,
O God, we offer ourselves to you,
  as your people have done before,
  as they still do everywhere.
Use us as you will
  that we may die to self to live for you.**

Accept us.
Accept what we have said and done here.
We have no right to ask this.
But Christ was born and died for us.
We ask it then in his name. Amen.

*The Lord's Prayer shall be said.*

Our Father in heaven,
   your name be hallowed,
   your kingdom come,
   your will be done,
   on earth as in heaven.
Give us today our daily bread.
Forgive us the wrong we have done,
   as we have forgiven those who have wronged us.
And do not bring us to the test
   but save us from evil.
For yours is the kingdom, the power and the glory
   forever. Amen.

*The minister shall take a large piece of bread, break it and say,*

The body of Christ broken for you.

*Then he shall take the cup and say,*

The blood of Christ shed for you.

*When the bread is given to the people the minister shall say,*

Jesus Christ, the bread of life.

*When the wine is given to the people the minister shall say,*

Jesus Christ, the true vine.

*What remains of the bread and wine shall be put back on the Table and covered.*

*A post-communion prayer shall be said by all.*

**For the bread we have eaten,**
**for the wine we have tasted,**
**for the life we have received,**
**we thank you, God.**

**Grant that what we have done**
**and have been given here**
**may so put its mark upon us**
**that it may remain always in our hearts.**
**Grant that we may become mature Christians,**
**that ours may be the faith which issues in action;**
**through Christ our Lord. Amen.**

*A hymn shall be sung.*

*A commissioning shall be given.*

Go into the world in the power of the Holy Spirit to fulfil your ministry as servants and soldiers of Jesus Christ.

*The service shall conclude with a blessing.*

The grace of the Lord Jesus Christ, and the love of God, and fellowship in the Holy Spirit be with you all. **Amen.**

ANOTHER OUTLINE FOR
## THE CELEBRATION OF
## THE LORD'S SUPPER

| | |
|---|---|
| *The Introduction* | Hymn |
| | Prayer of Approach |
| | Confession of Sin or Prayer of Supplication |
| | Litany |
| | Canticle or Hymn |
| | |
| *The Ministry of the Word* | Prayer for Grace |
| | Old Testament |
| | Epistle |
| | Psalm |
| | Gospel |
| | Hymn |
| | Announcements |
| | Sermon |
| | Creed or Te Deum |
| | Prayers of Intercession and Commemoration of the Dead |
| | |
| *The Holy Communion* | Offertory |
| | Hymn |
| | Invitation |
| | Confession of Sin |
| | Prayer for Pardon |
| | Comfortable Words |
| | Prayer of Humble Access |
| | Prayer of Thanksgiving and Consecration |
| | Lord's Prayer |
| | Fraction |
| | Distribution |
| | Prayers of Thanksgiving and Supplication |
| | Hymn |
| | Blessing |

AN ORDER FOR
## THE CELEBRATION OF
## THE LORD'S SUPPER
based on the foregoing outline

### The Introduction

*The service shall begin with a psalm or hymn showing forth the power, the goodness and the grace of God.*
*Then shall the minister pray in this wise, he and the people humbly seeking the mercy of God.*

Almighty God, unto whom all hearts be open, all desires known, and from whom no secrets are hid: cleanse the thoughts of our hearts by the inspiration of thy Holy Spirit, that we may perfectly love thee, and worthily magnify thy holy name; through Christ our Lord. **Amen.**

*Then the minister shall say,*

O Lord God, hear us when we make our common supplications unto thee. For the peace that is from above, and for the loving kindness of our God, we make our supplication unto thee.

For the peace of the whole world, for the well-being of the churches of God, and for the unity of them all, we make our supplication unto thee.

For this house of prayer, and for all that with faith, reverence, and the fear of God enter here, we make our supplication unto thee.

Remembering what thy love hath wrought in thy saints, and thy faithfulness to our fathers and brethren who are now with thee, we commend ourselves, and one another, and all our life, to Christ our Lord.

Help, save, pity, and defend us, O God, by thy grace. **Amen.**

*Then shall be sung or said this litany.*

**Lord, have mercy.**
**Christ, have mercy.**
**Lord, have mercy.**

*Then shall be sung or said Gloria in excelsis or Benedictus or a hymn of praise and humble gratitude to God.*

## The Ministry of the Word

*Then shall be said a prayer for grace.*

*Then shall be read a lesson from the Old Testament, or a lesson from an epistle, or both.*

*Here a psalm or part of a psalm may be sung or said.*

*Then shall a part of one of the Gospels be read.*

*Here a hymn may be sung.*

*Then the minister shall make such announcements as are needful and fitting.*

*Then shall follow a sermon.*

*A creed may be said or sung, or the hymn Te Deum may be sung.*

*Then shall follow intercession for the church, for the nation and for all men, and commemoration of the departed.*

## The Holy Communion

*Here the offerings of the people shall be collected and presented; and the bread and wine shall be prepared for the sacrament; and a psalm or hymn may be sung.*

*Here may be read the narrative of the institution of the Lord's Supper. If it is read at this point it shall be omitted from the prayer of thanksgiving and consecration.*

1 Corinthians 11. 23-26

I have received of the Lord that which also I delivered unto you, that the Lord Jesus the same night in which he was betrayed took bread: and when he had given thanks, he brake it, and said, Take, eat: this is my body, which is broken for you: this do in remembrance of me. After the same manner also he took the cup, when he had supped, saying, This cup is the new testament in my blood: this do ye, as oft as ye drink it, in remembrance of me. For as often as ye eat this bread, and drink this cup, ye do shew the Lord's death till he come.

*Then shall the minister say,*

Ye that do truly and earnestly repent of your sins, and are in love and charity with your neighbours, and intend to lead a new life, following the commandments of God, and walking from henceforth in his holy ways: draw near with faith, and take this holy sacrament to your comfort; and make your humble confession to almighty God.

*Then shall this general confession be said by the minister and all the people.*

**Almighty God,**
   **Father of our Lord Jesus Christ,**
   **Maker of all things,**
   **Judge of all men:**
**we acknowledge and confess our manifold sins**
   **which we, from time to time, have committed**
   **by thought, word and deed,**
   **against thy divine majesty.**

**We do earnestly repent,**
    **and are heartily sorry**
    **for these our misdoings.**
**Have mercy upon us,**
    **have mercy upon us, most merciful Father.**
**For thy Son our Lord Jesus Christ's sake**
    **forgive us all that is past,**
    **and grant that we may hereafter**
    **serve and please thee in newness of life**
    **to the honour and glory of thy name;**
    **through Jesus Christ our Lord. Amen.**

*Here the minister shall say,*

Almighty God, our heavenly Father, who of thy great mercy hast promised forgiveness of sins to all them that with hearty repentance and true faith turn unto thee: have mercy upon us; pardon and deliver us from all sins; confirm and strengthen us in all goodness; and bring us to everlasting life; through Jesus Christ our Lord. **Amen.**

*Here the minister shall say to the people,*

Hear what comfortable words our Saviour Christ saith unto all that truly turn to him.

Come unto me, all ye that labour and are heavy laden, and I will give you rest.     *Matthew 11.28*

God so loved the world, that he gave his only begotten Son, that whosoever believeth in him should not perish, but have everlasting life.

    *John 3.16*

Hear also what Saint Paul saith.

This is a true saying, and worthy of all acceptation, that Jesus Christ came into the world to save sinners.

*I Timothy 1. 15*

Hear also what Saint John saith.

If any man sin, we have an Advocate with the Father, Jesus Christ the righteous; and he is the propitiation for our sins.

*I John 2. 1, 2*

*Then shall the minister say,*

Let us pray.

We do not presume to come to this thy Table, O merciful Lord, trusting in our own righteousness, but in thy manifold and great mercies. We are not worthy so much as to gather up the crumbs under thy Table. But thou art the same Lord, whose property is always to have mercy: grant us therefore, gracious Lord, so to eat the flesh of thy dear Son Jesus Christ, and to drink his blood, that our sinful bodies may be made clean by his body, and our souls washed through his most precious blood, and that we may evermore dwell in him, and he in us. **Amen.**

*Then shall the minister say, and the people answer, as follows,*

*Minister.*

The Lord be with you;

*People.*

**And with thy spirit.**

*Minister.*

Lift up your hearts;

*People.*

**We lift them up unto the Lord.**

*Minister.*

Let us give thanks unto our Lord God;

*People.*

**It is meet and right so to do.**

*Then the minister, proceeding, shall say,*

It is very meet, right, and our bounden duty, that we should at all times, and in all places, give thanks unto thee, O holy Lord, Father almighty, everlasting God, who didst create the heavens and the earth and all that in them is, who didst make man in thine own image, and whose tender mercies are over all thy works.

*Here may follow one of the proper prefaces.*

*at Christmas*

And who didst give Jesus Christ thine only Son to be born for us, that by taking flesh of our humanity he might make us partakers of the divine glory.

*at Easter*

But chiefly are we bound to praise thee for the glorious resurrection of thy Son Jesus Christ our Lord; for he is the very Paschal Lamb, which was offered for us, and hath taken away the sin of the world; who by his death hath destroyed death, and by his rising to life hath begotten us again unto a living hope.

*at Pentecost*

And who didst pour forth upon the church thy Holy and life-giving Spirit: that through his power the everlasting gospel might go forth into all the world: whereby we have been brought out of darkness and error into the clear light and true knowledge of thee and of thy Son our Saviour Jesus Christ.

*And the minister shall continue thus,*

Therefore with angels and archangels and with all the company of heaven, we laud and magnify thy glorious name; evermore praising thee, and saying,

**Holy, holy, holy, Lord God of hosts,**
**heaven and earth are full of thy glory.**
**Glory be to thee, O Lord most high.**

*Here may the following anthem be sung or said.*

**Blessed is he that cometh in the name of the Lord:**
**hosanna in the highest.**

*And the minister shall continue thus,*

All glory and thanksgiving be to thee, almighty God, our heavenly Father, for that thou of thy tender mercy didst give thine only Son Jesus Christ to take our nature upon him, and to suffer death upon the Cross for our redemption; who made there a full, perfect, and sufficient sacrifice for the sins of the whole world; and did institute, and in his holy gospel, command us to continue, a perpetual memory of that his precious death until his coming again:

Who, the same night in which he was betrayed, took bread, and when he had given thanks, he brake it, and said, Take, eat, this is my body, which is broken for you; this do in remembrance of me. After the same manner also he took the cup, saying, This cup is the new covenant in my blood; this do ye, as oft as ye drink it, in remembrance of me.

Wherefore, having in remembrance his precious death and passion, his glorious resurrection and ascension, and pleading his eternal sacrifice, we thy servants do set forth this memorial which he hath willed us to make, giving thee thanks that thou hast counted us worthy to stand before thee.

And we most humbly beseech thee, O merciful Father, to vouchsafe unto us thy gracious presence, and so to sanctify with thy Word and Spirit these thine own gifts of bread and wine which we set before thee, that the bread which we break may be to us the communion of the body of Christ, and the cup of blessing which we bless the communion of the blood of Christ.

And we entirely desire thy fatherly goodness mercifully to accept this our sacrifice of praise and thanksgiving; most humbly beseeching thee to grant, that by the merits and death of thy Son Jesus Christ, we and thy whole church may obtain remission of our sins, and all other benefits of his passion.

And here we offer and present unto thee, O Lord, ourselves, our souls and bodies, to be a reasonable, holy, and living sacrifice unto thee; humbly beseeching thee, that all we, who are partakers of this Holy Communion, may be fulfilled with thy grace and heavenly benediction.

And although we be unworthy, through our manifold sins, to offer unto thee any sacrifice, yet we beseech thee to accept this our bounden duty and service, not weighing our merits, but pardoning our offences;

Through Jesus Christ our Lord, by whom, and with whom in the unity of the Holy Spirit, all honour and glory be unto thee, O Father almighty, world without end. **Amen.**

And now, as our Saviour Christ hath taught us, we say,

**Our Father, who art in heaven,**
   **hallowed be thy name,**
   **thy kingdom come,**
   **thy will be done,**
   **on earth as it is in heaven.**
**Give us this day our daily bread,**
   **and forgive us our trespasses**
   **as we forgive those who trespass against us,**
   **and lead us not into temptation**
   **but deliver us from evil.**
**For thine is the kingdom, the power and the glory,**
   **for ever and ever. Amen.**

*Then the minister shall say,*

According to the holy example of our Lord Jesus Christ, and in remembrance of him, we do this;

who, the same night in which he was betrayed, took bread;

*Here he shall take the bread in his hands.*

And when he had given thanks, he brake it,

*Here he shall break the bread.*

And said, Take, eat, this is my body which is broken for you; this do in remembrance of me.
After the same manner also he took the cup;

*Here he shall take the cup into his hands.*

Saying, This cup is the new covenant in my blood; this do ye, as oft as ye drink it, in remembrance of me.

*Then shall the minister say,*

The peace of the Lord Jesus Christ be with you all.

*Then shall the minister and people receive the communion.*

*This anthem may be sung when minister and people receive the communion.*

**O Lamb of God, who takest away the sin of the world, have mercy upon us.**

**O Lamb of God, who takest away the sin of the world, have mercy upon us.**

**O Lamb of God, who takest away the sin of the world, grant us thy peace.**

*When the minister delivers the bread, he shall say,*

The body of our Lord Jesus Christ, which was given for *thee,* preserve *thee* unto everlasting life. Take and eat this in remembrance that Christ died for *thee,* and feed on him in *thy* heart by faith with thanksgiving.

*And when the minister delivers the cup, he shall say,*

The blood of our Lord Jesus Christ, which was shed for *thee,* preserve *thee* unto everlasting life. Drink this in remembrance that Christ's blood was shed for *thee,* and be thankful.

*When all have communicated, what remains of the sacred elements shall be reverently placed upon the Table, and covered with a fair linen cloth.*

*Then shall the minister give thanks to God, and beseech his grace, in the name of all them that have communicated, saying,*

Heavenly Father, we give thee praise and thanks that upon us the unworthy thou dost confer so rich a benefit as to bring us into the communion of thy Son Jesus Christ; whom, having delivered up to death, thou hast given for our nourishment unto eternal life. Now also grant us grace, that we may never be unmindful of these things; but bearing them about, engraven on our hearts, may advance and grow in that faith which is effectual unto every good work; through Jesus Christ our Lord. **Amen.**

We remember before thee the multitude of every name who are joined with us throughout the world. O Lord, save thy people and bless thine inheritance; feed them also, and lift them up for ever. And we bless thy holy name for all thy servants who have finished their course, especially those dear to our own souls who have entered into thy rest. And rejoicing that we are still one with them in the same holy fellowship, we pray that we may be united with them in the joy and peace of the perfect life; through Jesus Christ our Lord. **Amen.**

*Where it is customary, a second offering, for benevolent purposes, may be taken.*

*Then may a hymn be sung.*

*Then shall the minister let the people depart with this blessing.*

The peace of God, which passeth all understanding, keep your hearts and minds in the knowledge and love of God, and of his Son Jesus Christ our Lord; and the blessing of God almighty, the Father, the Son, and the Holy Spirit, be amongst you and remain with you always. **Amen.**

AN ORDER FOR

## THE CELEBRATION OF
## THE LORD'S SUPPER

for use in the home or a small group

*During a study group, small meeting or fellowship meal, or at their close, the elements, which may have been previously in use, are placed before the minister. Customary and familiar dishes may be used.*

*Eucharistic passages such as the following may be read and, where desirable, shared in free discussion:*

The Experience of the Emmaus Road     *Luke 24. 30-35*

The Feeding of the Five Thousand     *Luke 9. 10-17*

The Parable of the Banquet of the Poor   *Luke 14. 15-24*

Jesus, the Bread of Life     *John 6. 25-34*

The Unity of Christians in the "One Loaf"

*I Corinthians 10. 14-21*

*There will follow festive prayers giving thanks for the continual action of the love of God in this world.*

*Recalling the whole ministry of Jesus, and remembering in particular the liberating triumph of his death and resurrection, the minister will celebrate the presence of the Holy Spirit active in the sharing of the bread and wine.*

*A prayer of dedication and response will follow. It will emphasize the offering of our lives, individually and together, by which we participate in the continuing ministry of Christ.*

*The minister will break the bread, pour the wine and lift up the cup while he says:*

The body of Christ broken for you.
The blood of Christ shed for you.

*or*

Every time you eat this bread and drink the cup,

you proclaim the death of the Lord, until he comes.

*or*

When we break the bread, it is a means of sharing in the body of Christ. When we bless 'the cup of blessing' it is a means of sharing in the blood of Christ.

Because there is one loaf, we, many as we are, are one body; for it is one loaf of which we partake.

*The bread may be shared by passing it from hand to hand, each breaking off a portion. The wine may be shared from a common cup or by pouring for each from a common pitcher.*

*When all have partaken, a prayer of thanksgiving for communion in Christ shall be said and intercessory prayer offered. These prayers may be in the form of biddings, with use of silence and of free and spontaneous participation by members of the group. It is desirable that the content be concrete and particular. These prayers should be focused on opportunities and responsibilities of ministry by the group for the upbuilding of the body of Christ throughout the world.*

*When desirable a hymn or doxology may be sung. The service should conclude with a commission and blessing.*

## 2. SERVICES OF INITIATION

### Introduction

In The United Church of Canada, by decision of the 20th General Council, the recommended sequence of admission to full membership is the traditional one of baptism, confirmation and first communion.

The orders of baptism and confirmation provided here are full orders of worship for the Lord's day, including all the elements contained in the regular order of public worship. With careful planning, they need not take much more time than the usual Sunday service.

### Infant Baptism

The normal practice of The United Church of Canada is to baptize publicly the children of believing parents who, themselves having been baptized and confirmed, bring their little ones before the church. Because the parents (or sponsors) take direct responsibility for the Christian training of the child, they take the vows.

The congregation stands for the vows, since they also sponsor the child and assume with the parents the responsibility for his Christian education and spiritual growth. The entire congregation fulfils the role of those who in some communions are designated as godparents.

### The Baptism and Confirmation of Adults

When the baptized child has come to years of discretion it is expected that he will stand before the church and make a responsible profession of his own faith. This implies that he has been carefully instructed.

Frequently men and women who have not been baptized as children come to profess their faith and to be received into full communion. Adult baptism and confirmation are one order and are so set forth here.

Although sprinkling and pouring are the usual methods of baptism in The United Church of Canada, those adults who request it may be baptized by immersion.

For members received from other congregations or communions an Order for the Welcoming of Members is provided (page 231). Those whose membership has lapsed should be received back into the church not by confirmation but by an Order for the Restoration of Members (page 234).

AN OUTLINE FOR

## THE BAPTISM OF CHILDREN

*The Approach*
Scripture Sentences
Prayer of Approach
Hymn
Confession of Sin
Assurance of Pardon
Doxology or Hymn

*The Word*
Prayer for Grace
Old Testament
Epistle
Psalm
Gospel
Hymn
Sermon
Prayer or Ascription
Banns and Announcements

*The Action*
Offertory
Hymn
Scripture Record and Teaching
Profession of Faith
Promises
Invocation of the Holy Spirit
Baptism
Declaration

*The Response*
Prayers of Thanksgiving and Intercession
Lord's Prayer
Hymn
Blessing

AN ORDER FOR
**THE BAPTISM OF CHILDREN**
based on the foregoing outline

## The Approach

*The people having assembled, the minister shall call them to worship with sentences appropriate to the season of the Christian Year, or one or both of the following,*

Thus says the Lord:
"Fear not, for I have redeemed you;
I have called you by name, you are mine." *Isa. 43.1*

If any one is in Christ, he is a new creation; the old has passed away, behold the new has come.

*II Corinthians 5. 17*

*A prayer of approach appropriate to the season of the Christian Year shall be said, or the following,*

O Lord our God, who hast commanded the light to shine out of darkness and hast called us to praise thee and to seek thy grace: accept this our sacrifice of worship; make us to be children of light and of the day and heirs of thine eternal inheritance; bestow thy mercy upon us, and grant that we may ever glorify thy holy name; through Jesus Christ our Lord. **Amen.**

*A hymn of praise shall be sung.*

*A prayer of confession shall be said by minister and people.*

**Almighty God,**
**Father of our Lord Jesus Christ,**
**Maker of all things,**
**Judge of all men:**
**we acknowledge and confess our manifold sins**
**which we, from time to time, have committed**
**by thought, word and deed,**
**against thy divine majesty.**
**We do earnestly repent,**
**and are heartily sorry**
**for these our misdoings.**
**Have mercy upon us,**
**have mercy upon us, most merciful Father.**
**For thy Son our Lord Jesus Christ's sake**
**forgive us all that is past,**
**and grant that we may hereafter**
**serve and please thee in newness of life**
**to the honour and glory of thy name;**
**through Jesus Christ our Lord. Amen.**

*The minister shall give an assurance of pardon.*

Hear words of scripture which declare forgiveness of sins.

If we confess our sins, he is faithful and just and will forgive our sins and cleanse us from all un-righteousness.

Therefore I assure you who turn to him in repentance and faith that God forgives you your sins.

*Then may be sung a doxology, or a suitable hymn of praise.*

**The Word**

*A prayer for grace appropriate to the season of the Christian Year shall be said, or the following,*

O God our Father, whose blessed Son Jesus Christ is the way, the truth and the life: enlighten us by thy word, empower us with thy Spirit and strengthen us in the faith into which we have been baptized; through the same Jesus Christ our Lord.

**Amen.**

*A lesson from the Old Testament, or from a book of the New Testament other than a gospel, or both, appropriate to the season of the Christian Year, shall be read.*

*A psalm or canticle shall be said or sung, with this conclusion wherever appropriate,*

**Glory be to the Father,**
   **and to the Son,**
   **and to the Holy Spirit;**
**as it was in the beginning,**
   **is now, and ever shall be:**
      **world without end. Amen.**

*A lesson from one of the gospels, appropriate to the season of the Christian Year, shall be read.*

*A hymn or anthem shall be sung.*

*A prayer for illumination may be said.*

Gracious God, who dost teach and guide thy people by thy holy word: show us thy truth, and reveal anew unto us the greatness of thy love; through Jesus Christ our Lord. **Amen.**

*A sermon shall be preached.*

*Prayer or an ascription shall follow.*

Now unto the God of all grace, who hath called us unto his eternal glory by Christ Jesus, be glory and dominion for ever and ever. **Amen.**

*The banns of marriage may be published and any necessary announcements shall be made.*

**The Action**

*The offerings of the people shall be collected and presented, and an offertory prayer said.*

O Lord our God, send down upon us thy Holy Spirit, we pray thee, to cleanse our hearts, to hallow our gifts, and to perfect the offering of ourselves to thee; through Jesus Christ our Lord. **Amen.**

*A hymn shall be sung, during which the children to be baptized shall be brought forward by their parents (or sponsors) and presented by an elder.*

*The minister shall say,*

Hear the command of the risen Christ.

All authority in heaven and on earth has been given me. Go therefore and make disciples of all nations, baptizing them in the name of the Father and of the Son and of the Holy Spirit, teaching them to observe all that I have commanded you; and lo, I am with you always, to the close of the age. *Matthew 28.18-20*

Hear also the record of our Lord's concern for children.

They were bringing children to Jesus, that he might touch them; and the disciples rebuked them. But when Jesus saw it he was indignant, and said to them, "Let the children come to me, do not hinder them; for to such belongs the kingdom of God. Truly I say to you, whoever does not receive the kingdom of God like a child shall not enter it." And he took them in his arms and blessed them, laying his hands upon them. *Mark 10.13-16*

*The minister shall say to the parents (or sponsors),*

In baptism we celebrate God's love,
> a love revealed in the life, death and resurrection of our Lord Jesus Christ,
> a love which has surrounded *this child* from *his* beginning.

In baptism we proclaim that God has acted to save *him*.
> He washes *him* in his cleansing waters and adopts *him* as a member of his family,
> incorporating *him* into the living body of Christ.

In baptism we dedicate *him* to God's purposes,
> knowing that even though we may falter, God will not,
>> that he will continue, through his Spirit, the work begun this day,
> a work in which life triumphs over death.

I ask therefore, do you present *this child,* earnestly desiring that by holy baptism *he* be made a *member* of the church of Christ?

*Answer.*

I do.

*The people shall rise and the minister shall say,*

Beloved in the Lord, do you receive *this child* in Christ's name as we have been received, promising to support *him* with constant love, wholesome example, Christian teaching and faithful prayer? Are you willing to accept so great a responsibility?

*Answer.*

**We are willing, God being our helper.**

*Then may the Apostles' Creed be said by all.*

*The minister shall say to the parents (or sponsors).*

I ask you before God and this congregation, do you profess your faith in God your heavenly Father, in Jesus Christ your Saviour and Lord, and in the Holy Spirit your Teacher and Guide?

*Answer.*

I do.

Will you bring up your child in the knowledge and love of God, teaching *him* the truths and duties of the Christian faith?

*Answer.*

I will, God being my helper.

Will you make a Christian home for *him,* so fashioning your lives that *he* may come to know Christ as *his* Lord and Saviour?

*Answer.*

I will, God being my helper.

Will you encourage *him* to seek confirmation, so that being strengthened in faith by the Holy Spirit and nurtured at the Table of the Lord, *he* may go forth to serve God faithfully in the world?

*Answer.*

I will, God being my helper.

*The people shall be seated and the minister shall say,*

Almighty and eternal God, whose beloved Son our Lord Jesus Christ has bidden us make disciples of all nations baptizing them in thy name: sanctify with thy Spirit, we pray thee, *this child* now to be baptized according to thy word; through Jesus Christ our Lord. **Amen.**

*The minister (taking the child in his arms, or leaving him in the arms of one of the parents or sponsors), shall say,*

What is the name of this child?

*Having named him, he shall sprinkle water on the head of the child, saying,*

N. *Christian names,* I baptize you in the name of the Father, and of the Son, and of the Holy Spirit. **Amen.**

*After those presented for baptism have been baptized the minister shall say,*

In the name of the Lord Jesus Christ, the King and head of the Church, I declare that N. *Christian names and surname* has now been received into the holy catholic church.

*And the following shall be said or sung.*

The Lord bless you and keep you: the Lord make his face to shine upon you, and be gracious unto you: the Lord lift up his countenance upon you, and give you peace. **Amen.**

## The Response

*Prayers of thanksgiving and intercession shall follow.*

All glory be unto thee, O Lord our heavenly Father, for the creation of the world, for the gift of life, for making man in thine own image and for thy love for all thy children.

All blessing be unto thee for sending thy Son Jesus Christ to redeem us from sin and death and to open to us the gate of life eternal.

All praise be unto thee for giving the Holy Spirit and for his work in thy Church and world to revive, uphold and guide us.

All thanksgiving be unto thee, O God, Father, Son and Holy Spirit, for this sacrament by which thou hast received *this child* into the family and household of faith, making *him* thine own. **Amen.**

Remember, O God, *this child,* that as *he* grows in knowledge of thy truth *he* may be led to acknowledge Jesus Christ as Lord and Saviour.

Remember, O God, the parents of *this child,* that they may be strengthened to keep the promises they have made and so to live that their *child* shall see in them what it means to follow Christ.

Remember, O God, all those who have not yet given themselves to Christ, that they may come to confess their faith and know the joy of salvation.

*Other prayers of intercession may be said.*

*Then the minister and people shall say,*

**Our Father, grant that we who have been baptized may be true to thee to our life's end. In thy great mercy unite us at the last with all thy children in the joy and glory of thine eternal kingdom. And to thee, Father, Son and Holy Spirit, be all blessing, praise and thanksgiving for ever and ever. Amen.**

*The Lord's Prayer shall be said by minister and people*

**Our Father, who art in heaven,**
**hallowed be thy name,**
**thy kingdom come,**
**thy will be done,**
**on earth as it is in heaven.**

**Give us this day our daily bread,**
**and forgive us our trespasses**
**as we forgive those who trespass against us,**
**and lead us not into temptation**
**but deliver us from evil.**
**For thine is the kingdom, the power and the glory,**
**for ever and ever. Amen.**

*A hymn shall be sung.*

*The minister shall dismiss the people with a blessing.*

The grace of the Lord Jesus Christ, and the love of God, and the fellowship of the Holy Spirit, be with you all. **Amen.**

*The sacrament of baptism will normally be administered in the presence of the congregation, following the order set out above. If, however, special circumstances require a shorter order, it is recommended that the order begin with a suitable approach, followed by the segment of the above order beginning,*

> *"A hymn shall be sung, during which the children to be baptized shall be brought forward by their parents (or sponsors) and presented by an elder."*

*and ending with the blessing of the child.*

> *"The Lord bless you and keep you: the Lord make his face to shine upon you, and be gracious unto you: the Lord lift up his countenance upon you, and give you peace. **Amen.**"*

*The service shall conclude with prayers of thanksgiving and intercession, the Lord's Prayer and a blessing.*

*In case of extreme urgency, it will be sufficient to name the child, sprinkling or pouring water on his head and saying,*

N. *Christian names,* I baptize you in the name of the Father, and of the Son and of the Holy Spirit. **Amen.**

If the sacrament of the Lord's supper is to be celebrated the dedication of the offering should be transferred from the place given in the above service, the following order being observed:

> after the blessing of the child a hymn shall be sung, the bread and wine prepared, an offertory prayer said and the minister shall proceed in the order for the celebration of the Lord's supper. The prayers of intercession shall be said after all have communicated.

It is desirable that a short order for the celebration of the Lord's supper be used.

ANOTHER ORDER FOR
**THE BAPTISM OF CHILDREN**
based on the foregoing outline

*The Scripture Sentences, Prayer of Approach, Prayer for Grace,
and Lessons, should be appropriate to the season of the
Christian Year.*

## The Approach

*Scripture Sentences*

God's promise was made to you and your children,
and to all who are far away — all whom the Lord
our God calls to himself.                    *Acts 2. 39*

When anyone is joined to Christ he is a new being:
the old is gone, the new has come.        *2 Cor. 5. 17*

*Prayer of Approach*

As on a first day you began the work of creating us;
as on a first day you raised your Son from the dead;
so on this first day, good Lord, freshen and remake
    us:
and as the week is new, let our lives begin again
because of Jesus who shows us your loving power.
                                   **Amen.**

*Hymn of Praise*

*Prayer of Confession*

**Father, we have sinned in many ways.**
**We have not loved you with all our hearts.**
**We have not loved one another as we should.**

**Sometimes we have let pride rule us,**
**sometimes anger;**
**sometimes our sin has been carelessness;**
**sometimes resentment, or impatience, or greed.**
**Forgive us.**
**We need your love.**

*Assurance of Pardon*

Here is good news:
Christ Jesus came that we might have life, life in all
    its fulness:
    to forgive us in our failure,
    to accept us as we are,
    to set us free from evil's power,
    to make us what we were meant to be.

*Doxology or Hymn of Praise*

**The Word**

*Prayer for Grace*

Father, in the gospel of Jesus Christ you have
assured us that we and our children are yours.
Give us the will to accept this heritage, and the
courage to grasp it; through Jesus Christ our Lord.
                          **Amen.**

*Lessons (from the Old Testament, or an Epistle, or both)*
*Psalm (with "Glory be to the Father")*
*Gospel*
*Hymn or Anthem*
*Sermon*
*Banns and Announcements*

**The Action**

*Offertory*

**God, you have given us life and its many resources. You have entrusted them to us to use wisely and unselfishly. Accept our gifts, and accept us; in Jesus' name we ask. Amen.**

*Hymn (during which the child to be baptized is brought forward by his parents (or sponsors) and presented by an elder.) The elder says:*

I present to you Mr. and Mrs. N. M. (or these parents) whose *child is* to be baptized.

*Statement (optional)*

After his resurrection Jesus said to his disciples: I have been given all authority in heaven and on earth. Go, then, to all peoples everywhere and make them my disciples; baptize them in the name of the Father and of the Son and of the Holy Spirit, and teach them to obey everything I have commanded you. And remember! I will be with you always, to the end of the age.          *Matthew 28. 18-20*

When people became Christians in the early church, they were baptized as Jesus had been; that is they went down under the water and came up again. This meant that they were dying to their old way of life and being born into a new life. Jesus made this possible by his own death and resurrection.

Although, in our tradition, people are seldom baptized by going down under the water, the meaning is the same. Baptism stands for the new life God gives us through Jesus. It proclaims that God has made us members of his family.

Today God calls   N. *Christian names*   (or *this child*) into this inheritance.

Since a child cannot understand what is being done, *his* parents and the church act on *his* behalf. The parents promise to bring *him* up in the Christian faith. We, the church, promise to help them. It is our hope and prayer that when *he* is old enough to understand, *he* will speak for *himself* and choose to be confirmed as one of Christ's people.

*Questions and Promises*

*(to the parents)*   Mr. and Mrs. N. M., you have brought your *son* here for baptism. Do you believe in God and in his love?

  Yes, we do.

Do you believe that God has made himself known to men in Jesus of Nazareth, who lived and died and lives again?

  Yes, we do.

Do you believe that God by his Spirit is active in the world to direct and strengthen you?

  Yes, we do.

Will you do your best to provide a Christian home for your *child,* and will you encourage *him* to seek confirmation?

Yes, we will.

*(the congregation stands)*

Do you, the members of this church, receive *this child* and promise to help in the Christian training of all children under your care?

**Yes, we do.**

Let us pray in silence for the gifts of God's Spirit.

*Baptism (minister takes the child in his arms).*

*(to the parents)*

What is the name of this child?

N. *Christian names*

N. *Christian names,* I baptize you in the name of the Father, and of the Son, and of the Holy Spirit.

**Amen.**

*Declaration and Blessing*

N. *Christian names and surname* has been received into the Christian church. May God bless you and keep you and give you peace.

## The Response

*Prayer of Thanksgiving*

**God of our fathers and of our children,**
**with joy we praise you,**
**we thank you, we honour you.**
**For your love which has made us and supports us,**
**we praise you.**
**For your gift of life embodied in these children,**
**we thank you.**

**For this sacrament by which they are received into
     your family, we honour you.
God of our fathers and of our children,
     with joy we praise you,
     we thank you, we honour you for ever.**

*Prayer of Intercession*

Father, keep *this child* in your truth as he grows in
mind and body. Keep these parents in your love as
they guide *their child* in the truth. Keep us also that
we may be faithful to you.

*Other Intercessions*

*Lord's Prayer*

**Our Father in heaven:
     holy be your name,
     your kingdom come,
     your will be done,
          on earth as in heaven.
     Give us today our daily bread.
     Forgive us our sins
          as we forgive those who sin against us.
     Save us in the time of trial,
          and deliver us from evil.
For yours is the kingdom, and the power,
          and the glory forever. Amen.**

*Hymn*

*Blessing*

The grace of the Lord Jesus Christ, and the love of
God, and fellowship in the Holy Spirit, be with
you all. **Amen.**

AN OUTLINE FOR

## ADULT BAPTISM AND CONFIRMATION

| | |
|---|---|
| *The Approach* | Scripture Sentences |
| | Prayer of Approach |
| | Hymn |
| | Confession of Sin |
| | Assurance of Pardon |
| | Doxology or Hymn |
| *The Word* | Prayer for Grace |
| | Old Testament |
| | Epistle |
| | Psalm |
| | Gospel |
| | Hymn |
| | Sermon |
| | Prayer or Ascription |
| | Banns and Announcements |
| *The Action* | Hymn |
| | Scripture Record and Teaching |
| | Profession of Faith |
| | Promises |
| | Invocation of the Holy Spirit |
| | Baptism |
| | Laying on of Hands |
| | Commissioning |
| | Reception |
| *The Response* | Offertory |
| | Prayers of Thanksgiving and Intercession |
| | Lord's Prayer |
| | Hymn |
| | Blessing |

AN ORDER FOR
## ADULT BAPTISM AND CONFIRMATION
based on the foregoing outline

### The Approach

*The candidates for confirmation being in the front pews, the minister shall call the people to worship with sentences appropriate to the season of the Christian Year or one or more of the following,*

They who wait for the Lord shall renew their strength, they shall mount up with wings like eagles, they shall run and not be weary, they shall walk and not faint.                    *Isaiah 40.31*

Wait for the Lord; be strong, and let your heart take courage; yea, wait for the Lord.    *Psalm 27.14*

The hour is coming, and now is, when the true worshippers will worship the Father in spirit and truth, for such the Father seeks to worship him.

*John 4.23*

*A prayer of approach appropriate to the season of the Christian Year, or the following, shall be said,*

Almighty and most gracious God, from whom comes every good and perfect gift: help us so to ask that we may receive, so to seek that we may find, so to knock that the door of thy mercy may be opened to us; through Jesus Christ our Lord.
                                        **Amen.**

*A hymn of praise shall be sung.*

*A prayer of general confession shall then be said by minister and people.*

**O God, Father, Son, and Holy Spirit,**
   **we confess to thee**
      **and to all the company of heaven**
      **and to one another**
   **that we have sinned**
      **in thought, word and deed,**
      **and by omission,**
         **through our fault, our own grievous fault.**

*Then the minister shall call the people to make their private confession of sin, saying,*

Let each of us in silence humbly confess his sins to almighty God.

*After a period of silence the following may be sung or said,*

**O Lamb of God, who takest away the sin of the world; have mercy upon us;**

**O Lamb of God, who takest away the sin of the world; have mercy upon us;**

**O Lamb of God, who takest away the sin of the world; grant us thy peace.**

*The minister shall give an assurance of pardon.*

Hear the good news and rejoice:

God so loved the world that he gave his only Son, that whoever believes in him should not perish, but have eternal life.

Therefore I assure you who turn to him in repentance and faith that God forgives you your sins.

*A doxology or suitable hymn of praise may be sung.*

### The Word

*A prayer for grace appropriate to the season of the Christian Year, or the following, shall be said,*

Almighty and ever blessed God, who hast given thy word to be a lamp unto our feet and a light unto our path: pour out upon us thy Holy Spirit that with humble and receptive hearts we may learn what thou wouldst have us do, and fashion our lives in obedience to thy holy will; through Jesus Christ our Lord. **Amen.**

*A lesson from the Old Testament, or from a book of the New Testament other than a gospel, or from both, appropriate to the season of the Christian Year, shall be read.*

*And one of the following psalms shall be sung or said,*

Psalm 27; Psalm 63; Psalm 119. 33-40

*After the psalm shall be sung or said,*

**Glory be to the Father,**
**and to the Son,**
**and to the Holy Spirit;**
**as it was in the beginning,**
**is now, and ever shall be:**
**world without end. Amen.**

*A lesson from one of the gospels appropriate to the season of the Christian Year shall be read.*

*A hymn shall be sung.*

*A sermon shall be preached.*

*A prayer or an ascription shall follow.*

Now to him who by the power at work within us is able to do far more abundantly than all we ask or think, to him be glory in the church and in Christ Jesus to all generations, for ever and ever. **Amen.**

*Banns of marriage may be published and such announcements as are needful and fitting shall be made.*

## The Action

*If there are no candidates for baptism the paragraphs marked \* shall be omitted.*

*A hymn shall be sung.*
*The minister shall say,*

\*Hear the record of the baptism of our Lord Jesus Christ and of the descent of the Holy Spirit upon him.

In those days Jesus came from Nazareth of Galilee and was baptized by John in the Jordan. And when he came up out of the water, immediately he saw the heavens opened and the Spirit descending upon him like a dove; and a voice came from heaven, "Thou art my beloved Son; with thee I am well pleased."

Mark 1.9-11

\*Hear the command of the risen Christ.
Jesus came and said to them, "All authority in heaven and on earth has been given to me. Go therefore and make disciples of all nations, baptizing them in the name of the Father and of the Son and of the Holy Spirit, teaching them to observe all that I have commanded you; and lo, I am with you always, to the close of the age."

Matthew 28.18-20

Hear the record of our risen Lord's gift of the Holy Spirit to his disciples.
Jesus said to them again, "Peace be with you. As the Father has sent me, even so I send you." And when he had said this, he breathed on them, and said to them, "Receive the Holy Spirit."

John 20.21, 22

Hear the record of the gift of the Holy Spirit to the church at Samaria.

Now when the apostles at Jerusalem heard that Samaria had received the word of God, they sent to them Peter and John, who came down and prayed for them that they might receive the Holy Spirit; for it had not yet fallen on any of them, but they had only been baptized in the name of the Lord Jesus. Then they laid their hands on them and they received the Holy Spirit.       *Acts 8.14-17*

*The minister shall say to the people,*

By baptism we are made members of the church of Jesus Christ and are adopted into the family and household of God.

When those who have been baptized as children have grown up and have been taught the essentials of Christian faith and duty they come before the church to own for themselves the covenant of their baptism. In this act they confess Jesus Christ openly as Saviour and Lord, that they may be confirmed by the Holy Spirit and welcomed to the Lord's Table.

*These same blessings of confirmation are also conferred upon those who not having been baptized as children do now confess Jesus Christ as Saviour and Lord and are through baptism received into his church.

*The people may stand and say the Apostles' Creed.*

*The candidates shall remain seated.*

*Then, the people standing, the clerk of session shall call the candidates by name (Christian name and surname). They shall rise and the minister shall say to them,*

I ask you before God and this congregation,

Do you profess your faith in God your heavenly Father, in Jesus Christ your Saviour and Lord, and in the Holy Spirit your Teacher and Guide?

*Answer.*
I do.

Will you be faithful in joining with the Lord's people in the worship of God, in studying the Bible and in prayer?

*Answer.*
I will, God being my helper.

Will you enter into the life and work of the church, supporting it with your gifts and sharing in its mission to all men?

*Answer.*
I will, God being my helper.

Will you endeavour daily to respond to God's love, to do his will, and to fulfil your Christian calling and ministry in the world?

*Answer.*
I will, God being my helper.

*Then the hymn* Come, Holy Ghost, our souls inspire *or* O Holy Spirit, by whose breath *may be sung.*

*The people shall be seated but the candidates shall remain standing. The minister shall say,*

Let us pray in silence that God in his loving kindness may pour out his Holy Spirit upon these his servants.

*Here silence shall be kept for a space, after which the minister shall say,*

Almighty and everlasting God, who of thine infinite mercy and goodness didst give Jesus Christ thy Son to be our Saviour; we pray thee to sanctify with thy Spirit thy servants who are to be (*baptized and) confirmed according to thy word; through the same Jesus Christ our Lord. **Amen.**

*The clerk of session shall summon by name each candidate for (*baptism and) confirmation.*

*\*A candidate to be baptized shall kneel at the font, and the minister shall sprinkle or pour water on his head, saying,*

*\*N. Christian names,* I baptize you in the name of the Father, and of the Son, and of the Holy Spirit.
**Amen.**

*\*After baptism the minister shall say,*

\*In the name of the Lord Jesus Christ, the King and Head of the Church, I declare that N. *Christian names and surname* is now received into the holy catholic church.

*The candidate kneeling, the minister shall lay hands upon his head and say,*

Confirm, O Lord, this thy servant N. *Christian names* by the Holy Spirit that *he* may continue thine forever.

*The people and the candidate shall say,*

**Amen.**

*The candidate shall rise and remain standing.*

*After each candidate has been confirmed the minister shall say to him,*

Go into the world in the power of the Holy Spirit to fulfil your high calling as a servant and soldier of Jesus Christ.

*And the clerk of session shall extend the right hand of fellowship.*

*After all the candidates have been confirmed they shall say together with the minister,*

Teach us, good Lord, to serve thee as thou deservest; to give and not to count the cost; to fight and not to heed the wounds; to toil and not to seek for rest; to labour and not to ask for any reward, save that of knowing that we do thy will; through the same Jesus Christ our Lord. **Amen.**

*The candidates shall return to their places in the congregation.*

### The Response

*The offerings of the people shall be collected.*

*The offerings shall be presented and an offertory prayer shall be said.*

O Lord God, Ruler of all things and Father of all men, accept, we pray, the offerings of thy people. Consecrate them by thy Spirit for the spread of thy gospel, and grant us willing hearts and ready hands to use all thy gifts to thy glory; through Jesus Christ our Lord. **Amen.**

*Prayers of thanksgiving and intercession shall follow.*

O Lord our God, all glory be unto thee for making us in thine own image and calling us to be stewards of thy good gifts.

All blessing be unto thee for sending thy Son Jesus Christ to redeem us from sin and death, and to open to us the gate of life eternal.

All thanksgiving be unto thee for giving the Holy Spirit and for his work in thy church and world to revive, uphold and guide us.

All praise and honour be unto thee, O God, Father, Son and Holy Spirit, for ever and ever. **Amen.**

Let us pray for the peace of the whole world, for the extension of God's kingdom and for the salvation of all men. *Silence.* Lord, hear our prayer:

*People.*
**And in thy love answer.**

*Minister.*
Let us pray for the well-being of the churches of God and for the unity of them all, that they may fulfil their mission in the world. *Silence.* Lord, hear our prayer:

*People.*
**And in thy love answer.**

*Minister.*
Les us pray for ministers of word and sacrament, for missionaries, for elders and teachers, and for all who bear office in the church, that they may be faithful to the work committed to them. *Silence.* Lord, hear our prayer:

*People.*
**And in thy love answer.**

*Minister.*

Let us pray for all who profess the name of Christ, and especially for those who this day have confessed him as Saviour and Lord, that they may be kept in the way of salvation. *Silence.* Lord, hear our prayer:

*People.*

**And in thy love answer.**

*Minister.*

Let us pray for the lonely and the troubled, for the sick and the sorrowful, and for those to whom death draws near, that they may be comforted. *Silence.* Lord, hear our prayer:

*People.*

**And in thy love answer.**

*Minister.*

Remembering what thy love has accomplished in thy saints, and thy faithfulness to those who have gone before us into thy presence, we commend ourselves and one another, and all our life, to Christ our Lord.

*People.*

**Help, save and strengthen us, O God, by thy grace.**
**Amen.**

*The Lord's Prayer shall be said by minister and people.*

**Our Father, who art in heaven,**
**  hallowed be thy name,**
**    thy kingdom come,**

**thy will be done,**
**on earth as it is in heaven.**
**Give us this day our daily bread,**
**and forgive us our trespasses**
**as we forgive those who trespasss against us,**
**and lead us not into temptation,**
**but deliver us from evil.**
**For thine is the kingdom, the power and the glory,**
**for ever and ever. Amen.**

*A hymn shall be sung.*

*The minister shall dismiss the people with a blessing.*

The Lord bless and keep you: the Lord make his face to shine upon you, and be gracious to you: the Lord lift up his countenance upon you, and give you peace. And the grace of the Lord Jesus Christ and the love of God and the fellowship of the Holy Spirit be with you all. **Amen.**

*If the sacrament of the Lord's supper is to be celebrated, in place of THE RESPONSE shall be inserted THE WORD OF GOD ENACTED from an order for the celebration of the Lord's supper. Prayers of intercession shall be included in the post-communion prayers.*

*If there are any to be received by transfer or certificate this may be done after the announcements have been made.*

ANOTHER ORDER FOR
## ADULT BAPTISM AND CONFIRMATION
based on the foregoing outline

*The Scripture Sentences, Prayer of Approach, Prayer for Grace, and Lessons, should be appropriate to the season of the Christian Year.*

### The Approach

*Scripture Sentence*

Since Jesus was delivered to you as Christ and Lord, live your lives in union with him. Be rooted in him; be built in him; be consolidated in the faith you were taught; let your hearts overflow with thankfulness. *Colossians 2. 6, 7*

*Prayer of Approach*

How generous you are, God.
You give good gifts to men.
Give us freedom to ask;
   give us openness to receive;
   may our search for fullness of life be satisfied,
   through Jesus Christ our Lord. **Amen.**

*Hymn of Praise*
*Confession*

**We confess we have not been honest with you, God,**
   **we have not been honest with each other.**
**We think, speak and act in ways that deny love:**
   **we put self first;**
   **we speak to hurt;**
   **we turn our back on need.**
**Forgive us.**

*(Silent Confession)*

*Assurance of Pardon*

Here is good news!

God loved the world so much that he gave his only Son, that everyone who has faith in him may not die but have eternal life.

Trust him, and you shall have new life.

Thanks be to God.

## The Word

*Prayer for Grace*

O living Word,
> in a world of many voices you define what is important.

Give us insight to know what to do;
> give us strength to do it. **Amen.**

*Lessons (from the Old Testament, or an Epistle, or both)*

*Psalm (with "Glory be to the Father")*

*Gospel*

*Hymn or Anthem*

*Sermon*

*Banns and Announcements*

## The Action

*(If there are no candidates for baptism omit the paragraphs marked \*.)*

*Hymn*

*Scripture Record and Teaching*

\*This is what the Gospel says of Jesus' own baptism: Jesus came from Nazareth, in the region of Galilee, and John baptized him in the Jordan. As soon as

Jesus came up out of the water he saw heaven opening and the Spirit came down on him like a dove. And a voice came from heaven: "You are my own dear Son, I am well pleased with you."

*Mark 1. 9-11*

\*After his resurrection Jesus said to his disciples:

I have been given all authority in heaven and on earth. Go, then, to all peoples everywhere and make them my disciples: baptize them in the name of the Father and of the Son and of the Holy Spirit, and teach them to obey everything I have commanded you. And remember! I will be with you always, to the end of the age. *Matthew 28. 18-20*

When Jesus gave the Holy Spirit to his disciples, after the resurrection, he said to them:

Peace be with you. As the Father sent me, so I send you. He said this, and then he breathed on them and said, Receive the Holy Spirit. *John 20.22*

In Acts we have an account of the gift of the Holy Spirit to the church at Samaria:

The apostles in Jerusalem heard that the people of Samaria had received the word of God; so they sent Peter and John to them. When they arrived, they prayed for the believers that they might receive the Holy Spirit. For the Holy Spirit had not yet come down on any of them; they had only been baptized in the name of the Lord Jesus. Then Peter and John placed their hands on them, and they received the Holy Spirit. *Acts 8. 14-17*

*(The minister may say to the people)*

In baptism we celebrate a new beginning. We are received into the Church. In Christ God says 'Yes' to us.

In confirmation we respond with 'Yes' to God, and we proclaim that God alone makes the difference to human life.

In confirmation we are strengthened by the Holy Spirit; we are welcomed to Christ's table; and we are commissioned to serve in the world.

*A Creed (optional)*

*An elder presents the candidates. He says*

I present to you   N. *Christian names and surnames*   for *baptism and confirmation.

*Questions and Promises (to the candidates)*

Do you believe in God and in his love?

>Yes, I do.

Do you believe that God has made himself known to men in Jesus of Nazareth, who lived and died and lives again?

>Yes, I do.

Do you believe that God by his Spirit is active in the world to direct and strengthen you?

>Yes, I do.

Do you commit yourself to God, Father, Son, and Spirit, to be his for ever?

>Yes, I do.

Will you meet regularly to celebrate his presence and discern his truth?

Yes, I will.

Will you act responsibly in your private and public life?

Yes, I will.

Will you take an active part in Christ's service to all men?

Yes, I will.

Let us pray in silence for the gifts of God's Spirit.

*\*Baptism (candidate kneeling)*

N. *Christian names* I baptize you in the name of the Father, and of the Son, and of the Holy Spirit.

**Amen.**

*\*Declaration*

N. *Christian names and surname* has been received into the Christian Church.

*Laying on of Hands*

By the gift of your Spirit, God, strengthen N. *Christian names* that *he* may be true to you all *his* life.

*Commissioning*

Go out into the world in the power of the Spirit. Pursue justice, faith, love, fortitude and humility. For to this you were called. *I Timothy 6. 11-12*

*(The candidates shall say in unison)*

Help me, Lord, to accept my calling and to live my faith in every part of life.

**The Response**

*Offertory Prayer*

**We bring our gifts to you, O God.**
**Here is the labour of our hands.**
**Here is the love of our hearts.**
**Accept them and use them;**
**through Christ our Lord. Amen.**

*Prayer of Thanksgiving*

**God of the heavens and the earth,**
   **with joy we praise you,**
   **we thank you, we honour you.**

**Because you have made us like yourself,**
   **made us to be creative in your world,**
   **we praise you.**

**Because you have given Jesus to set us free,**
   **given us courage to be,**
   **we thank you.**

**Because your Spirit is present with us,**
   **present to guide and renew,**
   **we honour you.**

**God of the heavens and the earth,**
   **with joy we praise you,**
   **we thank you, we honour you for ever.**

*(Prayers of intercession including a prayer for those who have been confirmed and concluding with a remembrance of the dead shall be said.)*

*Lord's Prayer*

**Our Father in heaven:**
**holy be your name,**
**your kingdom come,**
**your will be done,**
**on earth as in heaven.**
**Give us today our daily bread.**
**Forgive us our sins**
**as we forgive those who sin against us.**
**Save us in the time of trial,**
**and deliver us from evil.**
**For yours is the kingdom, and the power,**
**and the glory forever. Amen.**

*Hymn*

*Blessing*

The grace of the Lord Jesus Christ, and the love of God, and fellowship in the Holy Spirit, be with you all. **Amen.**

## 3. ORDERS FOR PUBLIC WORSHIP

### Introduction

Throughout most of the history of the Christian church a basic principle has governed the structure of public worship. The principle is simply that sermon and supper belong together as the full diet of public worship. Where it is not possible to celebrate the Lord's supper every week, the principle, nonetheless, governs the structure.

The First Order for Public Worship follows a simple pattern. The Approach to God: hymn of praise, scripture sentences, prayer of approach, confession, assurance of pardon; The Word of God: scripture lessons, psalm, hymn, and sermon; The Response of the people: the offering, prayers of thanksgiving and prayers for others. This structure follows closely the natural theological progression of God's initiative and man's response. When the communion elements are present, the thanksgiving prayer is the great communion prayer, but the shape of the service remains the same. This shape is found in most of the other services in this book.

The Second Order for Public Worship recognizes in its shape the fact that in The United Church of Canada we hold a wide diversity of traditions, one major stream of which comes from Anglicanism through Methodism and Congregationalism. In this order, the structure is based on the service of Morning Prayer, which itself developed in England as a condensation of the many daily prayer services of the monasteries. These services were compressed into two — one for morning prayer and one for evening prayer. A sermon was later added. They were never intended to have a celebration of the Lord's supper as an integral part of their structure. This pattern of worship is deeply embedded in the tradition of the four denominations which make up The United Church of Canada and has served as a vehicle of our public worship for a long time.

With the wide diversity of backgrounds and traditions in our church, with the different requirements of rural, urban and suburban congregations, with the diversity of gifts to be found in these congregations, and with the continuing principle of common order, not common prayer, the Orders for Public Worship have been drafted in skeletal form only, leaving to each congregation the freedom to work out prayers, hymns, lessons and responses that best suit its needs, within a reasonable and logical framework.

A large selection of calls to worship, invocations and prayers of all kinds may be found in this book in the section, Material for Services of Worship. The page numbers marked in the orders refer to that section.

These helps, together with the long tradition of free prayer, the Bible, and the hymn book will, it is hoped, make possible the expression of devotion to God in a manner helpful to each congregation of our church.

FIRST ORDER FOR
**PUBLIC WORSHIP**

**The Approach**

### Organ Prelude

> *The people may be called to worship with the playing of a suitable prelude.*

### Processional Hymn

> *When there is a processional, the hymn shall be a song of praise proclaiming the majesty, glory and grace of God.*

### Scripture Sentences

Pages 85-95   *Here may be said or sung sentences from Scripture appropriate to the season of the Christian Year or other special occasion.*

### Prayer of Approach

Pages 95-105   *A prayer of invocation or adoration, appropriate to the season of the Christian Year or other special occasion, shall be said.*

### Hymn of Praise

> *When there is not a processional, a hymn of praise proclaiming the majesty, glory and grace of God shall be sung here.*

### General Confession

Pages 105-112   *A prayer of general confession of sin shall then be said by minister and people.*

### Private Confession

> *The minister shall call the people to make their private confession of sin.*

### Litany

> *After a period of silence, the following may be sung or said,*

**Lord have mercy.**
**Christ have mercy.**
**Lord have mercy.**

## Assurance of Pardon

Pages 112-114     *The minister shall give an assurance of pardon.*

## Doxology

*Then may be sung a doxology or a suitable hymn of praise.*

### The Word of God

## Prayer for Grace

Pages 114-130     *A prayer for grace, appropriate to the season of the Christian Year and in keeping with the lessons that follow, shall be said.*

## Old Testament
## Epistle

Pages 256-265     *A lesson from the Old Testament, or from a book in the New Testament other than a gospel, or from both, appropriate to the season of the Christian Year, shall be read.*

## Psalm

Pages 256-265     *A psalm or canticle shall be sung or said, with this conclusion wherever appropriate*

**Glory be to the Father,
    and to the Son,
    and to the Holy Spirit;
as it was in the beginning,
    is now, and ever shall be:
        world without end. Amen.**

## Gospel

Pages 256-265     *A lesson from one of the gospels appropriate to the season of the Christian Year shall be read.*

## Hymn

*A hymn may be sung.*

## Sermon

*A sermon shall be preached.*

## Ascription

Pages 133-135    *An ascription of glory, a suitable prayer, or a period of silence, shall follow.*

## Hymn

*A hymn may be sung.*

## The Response

### Announcements

*Banns of marriage may be published, and any necessary announcements shall be made.*

### Offering (Anthem)

*The offerings of the people shall be collected; and a suitable anthem may be sung.*

### Offertory Prayer

Pages 135-138    *The offerings shall be presented and an offertory prayer shall be said.*

### Prayers

Pages 139-185    *Prayers of thanksgiving and intercession, with commemoration of the dead, shall follow.*

### Lord's Prayer

*The Lord's Prayer shall be said by minister and people.*

### Hymn

*A hymn shall be sung.*

### Commissioning

Pages 185-186

### Blessing

Pages 187-188    *The minister shall dismiss the people with a blessing.*

### Organ Postlude

## SECOND ORDER FOR
## PUBLIC WORSHIP

### Organ Prelude

> *The people may be called to worship with the playing of a suitable prelude.*

### Processional Hymn

> *When there is a processional, the hymn shall be a song of praise proclaiming the majesty, glory and grace of God.*

### Scripture Sentences

Pages 85-95    *Here may be said or sung sentences from Scripture appropriate to the season of the Christian Year or other special occasion.*

### Prayer of Approach

Pages 95-105    *A prayer of invocation or adoration, appropriate to the season of the Christian Year or other special occasion, shall be said.*

### Hymn of Praise

> *When there is not a processional, a hymn of praise proclaiming the majesty, glory and grace of God shall be sung here.*

### General Confession

Pages 105-112    *A prayer of general confession of sin shall be said by minister and people.*

### Assurance of Pardon

Pages 112-114    *The minister shall give an assurance of pardon.*

### Old Testament
### Epistle

Pages 256-265    *A lesson from the Old Testament, or from a book in the New Testament other than a gospel, or from both, appropriate to the season of the Christian Year, shall be read.*

## Psalm

Pages 256-265    *A psalm or canticle shall be sung or said, with this conclusion wherever appropriate,*

**Glory be to the Father,**
    **and to the Son,**
    **and to the Holy Spirit;**
**as it was in the beginning,**
    **is now, and ever shall be:**
        **world without end. Amen.**

## Gospel

Pages 256-265    *A lesson from one of the gospels appropriate to the season of the Christian Year shall be read.*

## Prayers

Pages 139-185    *Prayers of thanksgiving and intercession, with commemoration of the dead, shall follow.*

## Lord's Prayer

*The Lord's Prayer shall be said by minister and people.*

## Announcements

*Banns of marriage may be published, and any necessary announcements shall be made.*

## Offering (Anthem)

*The offerings of the people shall be collected, and a suitable anthem may be sung.*

## Offertory Prayer

Pages 135-138    *The offerings shall be presented and an offertory prayer shall be said.*

## Hymn

*A hymn shall be sung.*

## Sermon

*A sermon shall be preached.*

## Ascription

*An ascription of glory, a suitable prayer, or a period of silence, shall follow*

## Hymn

*A hymn shall be sung.*

## Commissioning

## Blessing

*The minister shall dismiss the people with a blessing.*

## Organ Postlude

# II. MATERIAL FOR SERVICES OF WORSHIP

## Introduction

This section provides material which may be used to fill out the orders for public worship. The examples of contemporary and traditional prayers are arranged in sub-sections to fit into the orders for public worship.

No attempt has been made to provide an exhaustive collection of material. Examples or models which may assist ministers and people in writing their own prayers relevant to the particular situation are given.

# 1. SCRIPTURE SENTENCES

**Season of Creation**

The earth is the Lord's and the fulness thereof,
the world and those who dwell therein. *Psalm 24.1*

Our help is in the name of the Lord,
who made heaven and earth. *Psalm 124.8*

He sends forth his command to the earth;
he makes his wind blow and the waters flow.
Praise the Lord. *Psalm 147.15, 18*

*Minister.*
Praise the Lord from the heavens,
praise him in the heights!
Praise him, sun and moon,
praise him, all you shining stars!

*People.*
His name alone is exalted;
his glory is above earth and heaven.
*Psalm 148.1-3, 13*

Jesus said, "Heaven and earth will pass away, but
my words will not pass away." *Mark 13.31*

Worthy art thou, our Lord and God,
to receive glory and honour and power,
for thou didst create all things,
and by thy will they existed and were created.
*Revelation 4.11*

**Harvest Thanksgiving**

While the earth remains, seedtime and harvest, cold and heat, summer and winter, day and night, shall not cease. *Genesis 8.22*

**All Saints' Day**

Since we are surrounded by so great a crowd of witnesses, let us lay aside every weight, and sin which clings so closely, and let us run with perseverance the race that is set before us, looking to Jesus the pioneer and perfecter of our faith.

*Hebrews 12.1, 2*

**Church Anniversary**

One generation shall laud thy works to another, and shall declare thy mighty acts. *Psalm 145.4*

**Sundays Before Christmas**

Our soul waits for the Lord; he is our help and shield. *Psalm 33.20*

In the wilderness prepare the way of the Lord, make straight in the desert a highway for our God.
And the glory of the Lord shall be revealed, and all flesh shall see it together, for the mouth of the Lord has spoken.

*Isaiah 40.3, 5*

Sing and rejoice, O daughter of Zion; for lo, I come and I will dwell in the midst of you, says the Lord. *Zechariah 2.10*

Repent, for the kingdom of heaven is at hand.

*Matthew 3.2*

Let your loins be girded and your lamps burning, and be like men who are waiting for their master.

*Luke 12.35*

Behold, the farmer waits for the precious fruits of the earth. You also be patient. Establish your hearts, for the coming of the Lord is at hand.

*James 5.7, 8*

## Christmas Eve

The glory of the Lord shall be revealed,
    and all flesh shall see it together,
      for the mouth of the Lord has spoken.   *Isaiah 40.5*

## Christmas Day

Behold, I bring you good news of a great joy which will come to all the people; for to you is born this day in the city of David a Saviour, who is Christ the Lord.

*Luke 2.10*

Glory to God in the highest,
    and on earth peace among men with whom he
    is pleased.

*Luke 2.14*

*Minister.*

To us a child is born, to us a Son is given; and the government will be upon his shoulder.

*People.*

His name will be called "Wonderful Counsellor, Mighty God, Everlasting Father, Prince of Peace."

*Isaiah 9.6*

**Sundays After Christmas**

> Arise, shine; for your light has come,
>     and the glory of the Lord has risen upon you.
>
>                                                           *Isaiah 60.1*

> It is God who said, "Let light shine out of darkness," who has shone in our hearts to give the light of the knowledge of the glory of God in the face of Christ.                    *II Corinthians 4.6*

> The Word became flesh and dwelt among us, full of grace and truth; we have beheld his glory, glory as of the only Son from the Father.       *John 1.14*

> The Lord is near to all who call upon him,
>     to all who call upon him in truth.
> He fulfils the desire of all who fear him,
>     he also hears their cry and saves them.
>
>                                                    *Psalm 145.18, 19*

**Old Year**

> The steadfast love of the Lord is from everlasting
>     to everlasting
>     upon those who fear him,
>     and his righteousness to children's children.
>
>                                                       *Psalm 103.17*

> The Lord will keep
>     your going out and your coming in
>     from this time forth and for evermore.
>
>                                                        *Psalm 121.8*

**New Year**

> Be strong and of good courage, do not fear or be in dread: for it is the Lord your God who goes with you; he will not fail you or forsake you.
>
>                                                    *Deuteronomy 31.6*

"I am the Alpha and the Omega," says the Lord God, who is and who was and who is to come, the Almighty.
*Revelation 1.8*

### Week of Prayer for Christian Unity

Behold, how good and pleasant it is
when brothers dwell together in unity!
*Psalm 133.1*

Jesus Christ came and preached peace to you who were far off and peace to those who were near; for through him we both have access in one Spirit to the Father.
*Ephesians 2.17, 18*

### Sundays Before Easter

The sacrifice acceptable to God is a broken spirit;
a broken and contrite heart, O God, thou wilt
not despise.
*Psalm 51.17*

Thou, O Lord, art a God merciful and gracious,
slow to anger and abounding in steadfast love
and faithfulness.
*Psalm 86.15*

Let us test and examine our ways,
and return to the Lord!
*Lamentations 3.40*

"Yet even now," says the Lord,
"return to me with all your heart,
and rend your hearts and not your garments."
Return to the Lord, your God,
for he is gracious and merciful,
slow to anger, and abounding in steadfast love.
*Joel 2.12, 13*

Jesus told his disciples, "If any man would come after me, let him deny himself and take up his cross and follow me."
*Matthew 16.24*

### Palm Sunday

Blessed be he who comes in the name of the Lord! Hosanna in the highest.
*Matthew 21.9*

### Good Friday

He was wounded for our transgressions,
 he was bruised for our iniquities;
 upon him was the chastisement that made us whole,
  and with his stripes we are healed.
*Isaiah 53.5*

Jesus said, "Now is the judgment of this world, now shall the ruler of this world be cast out; and I, when I am lifted up from the earth, will draw all men to myself."
*John 12.31, 32*

God shows his love for us in that while we were yet sinners Christ died for us.
*Romans 5.8*

### Easter Day

*Minister.*
The Lord is risen.
*People.*
He is risen indeed.
*Choir.*
Alleluia.
*Luke 24.34 (adapted)*

Jesus said, "I am the resurrection and the life; he who believes in me, though he die, yet shall he live, and whoever lives and believes in me shall never die."
*John 11.25, 26*

We know that Christ being raised from the dead will never die again; death no longer has dominion over him.
*Romans 6.9*

## Sundays After Easter

O sing to the Lord a new song,
　　for he has done marvellous things!
His right hand and his holy arm
　　have gotten him victory.
*Psalm 98.1*

The Lord has made known his victory
　　he has revealed his vindication in the sight of
　　the nations.
*Psalm 98.2*

Thanks be to God, who gives us the victory through our Lord Jesus Christ.
*I Corinthians 15.57*

Fear not, I am the first and the last, and the living one; I died, and behold I am alive for evermore.
*Revelation 1.17, 18*

## Ascension

Let the heavens be glad, and let the earth rejoice,
　　and let them say among the nations, "The Lord
　　reigns!"
*I Chronicles 16.31*

Since we have a great high priest who has passed through the heavens, Jesus, the Son of God, let us with confidence draw near to the throne of grace, that we may receive mercy and find grace to help in time of need.
*Hebrews 4.14, 16*

## Day of Pentecost

It shall come to pass afterward,
　　that I will pour out my spirit on all flesh.
*Joel 2.28*

*Minister.*

The hour is coming, and now is, when the true worshippers will worship the Father in spirit and truth, for such the Father seeks to worship him;

*People.*

God is spirit, and those who worship him must worship in spirit and truth. *John 4.23, 24*

You shall receive power when the Holy Spirit has come upon you; and you shall be my witnesses in Jerusalem and in all Judea and Samaria and to the end of the earth. *Acts 1.8*

God's love has been poured into our hearts through the Holy Spirit which has been given to us. *Romans 5.5*

### Sundays After Pentecost

*Minister.*

Holy, holy, holy, is the Lord of hosts;

*People.*

The whole earth is full of his glory. *Isaiah 6.3*

They who wait for the Lord shall renew their
strength;
they shall mount up with wings like eagles,
they shall run and not be weary,
they shall walk and not faint. *Isaiah 40.31*

*Minister.*

All the ends of the earth shall remember
and turn to the Lord;
and all the families of the nations
shall worship before him.

*People.*
Dominion belongs to the Lord,
   and he rules over the nations.     *Psalm 22.27, 28*

Serve the Lord with gladness!
Come into his presence with singing!
Enter his gates with thanksgiving,
   and his courts with praise!
Give thanks to him, bless his name!
For the Lord is good;
   his steadfast love endures for ever,
   and his faithfulness to all generations.
                              *Psalm 100.2, 4, 5*

Jesus said, "Lo, I am with you always, to the close
of the age."                         *Matt. 28.20*

**Dominion or National Day**

Blessed is the nation whose God is the Lord.
                              *Psalm 33.12*
Righteousness exalts a nation,
   but sin is a reproach to any people.    *Proverbs 14.34*

**Sunday before Labour Day**

*Minister.*
Unless the Lord builds the house,
   those who build it labour in vain.
*People.*
Unless the Lord watches over the city,
   the watchman stays awake in vain.     *Psalm 127.1*

**General**

Lift up your heads, O gates!
   and be lifted up, O ancient doors!
   that the King of glory may come in.     *Psalm 24.7*

Wait for the Lord;
  be strong, and let your heart take courage;
  yea, wait for the Lord!                    *Psalm 27.14*

O magnify the Lord with me,
  and let us exalt his name together!        *Psalm 34.3*

*Minister.*
O come, let us sing to the Lord;
*People.*
let us make a joyful voice to the rock of our salva-
  tion!
*Minister.*
Let us come into his presence with thanksgiving;
*People.*
let us make a joyful noise to him with songs of
  praise!                                   *Psalm 95.1, 2*

O worship the Lord in the beauty of holiness.
                                            *Psalm 96.9*

O give thanks to the Lord, for he is good;
  his steadfast love endures for ever!       *Psalm 107.1*

This is the day which the Lord has made;
  let us rejoice and be glad in it.          *Psalm 118.24*

Seek the Lord while he may be found,
  call upon him while he is near;
let the wicked forsake his way,
  and the unrighteous man his thoughts;
let him return to the Lord, that he may have mercy
  on him,
  and to our God, for he will abundantly pardon.
                                            *Isaiah 55.6, 7*

With what shall I come before the Lord,
    and bow myself before God on high?
He has showed you, O man, what is good;
    and what does the Lord require of you
but to do justice, and to love kindness,
    and to walk humbly with your God?

*Micah 6.6, 8*

Jesus said, "Ask, and it will be given you; seek and
you will find: knock, and it will be opened to you."

*Matthew 7.7*

## 2. PRAYERS OF APPROACH

### Season of Creation

Blessed be thou, Lord God our Father, for ever and
ever. Thine, O Lord, is the greatness and the might
and the glory and the victory and the majesty; for
all that is in the heavens and in the earth is thine;
thine is the kingdom, and thou art exalted as head
above all.
Wherefore we adore thee now and always. **Amen.**

As on a first day you began the work of creating us;
as on a first day you raised your Son from the dead;
so on this first day, good Lord, freshen and remake
    us:
and as the week is new, let our lives begin again
because of Jesus who shows us your loving power.

**Amen.**

Our God, how great you are! On the first day of
the week we commemorate your creation of the
world and all that is in it.

Thank you for the light which wakes us
morning by morning, and for that greater
light which shines in Jesus Christ.

Our God, how great you are! On the first day of
the week you raised Jesus from the dead.

Raise us with him to a new quality of faith and
life.

Our God, how great you are! Again on the first day
of the week you sent your Spirit on your
disciples.

Do not deprive us of your Spirit, but renew
him in us day by day. **Amen.**

Lord our God, great, eternal, wonderful, utterly to
be trusted: you give life to us all, you help those
who come to you, you give hope to those who
appeal to you. Set our hearts and consciences at
peace, so that we may bring our prayers to you
confidently and without fear; through Jesus Christ
our Lord. **Amen.**

### All Saints' Day

O eternal Lord God, who art worshipped and
adored by all the host of heaven: we join our
thanks and praise with the triumph song of prophets and apostles, saints and martyrs, beseeching
thee that we, who are unworthy, may by thy grace
be enabled to worship thee on earth; through
Jesus Christ our Lord. **Amen.**

## Sundays Before Christmas

O thou who art beyond our sight, above our thought, infinite, eternal, and unsearchable: thy wisdom shines in all thy works, thy glory is shown in thy goodness to men, and thy grace and truth are revealed in Christ. Therefore we adore thee, our Father and our God, for ever and ever. **Amen.**

Lord God almighty, King of glory and Love eternal, worthy art thou at all times to receive adoration, praise and blessing, but especially at this time do we praise thee for the sending of thy Son our Saviour Jesus Christ, for whom our hearts do wait, and to whom with thee and the Holy Spirit, one God, be honour and dominion, now and forever.
**Amen.**

## Christmas

O God, who loved us so much that you came to us as a man, we celebrate this day the coming of Jesus into our world. We remember before you his humble birth that lifts up all who are humbly born and puts down the proud and the arrogant. Give us the grace now to worship you in his spirit that this same love and humility may rule our hearts and govern our actions; through the same Jesus Christ our Lord. **Amen.**

O Lord our God, who didst manifest thy love toward us by sending thine only begotten Son in the world, that we might live through him: grant us, by thy Holy Spirit, the precious gift of faith, whereby we may know that the Son of God has come; and help us to join our praises with the song of the heavenly host: Glory to God in the highest, and on earth peace, good will toward men. **Amen.**

### Sundays After Christmas

O God, who by the shining of a star didst guide the wise men to behold thy Son our Lord: show us thy heavenly light and give us grace to follow until we find him and, finding him, rejoice. And grant that, as they presented gold, frankincense and myrrh, we now may bring him the offering of a loving heart, an adoring spirit and an obedient will, for his honour, and for thy glory, O God most high.
**Amen.**

Eternal God, who hast shined in our hearts to give the knowledge of thy glory in the face of Jesus Christ, grant us now such knowledge of thy grace that we may worship and adore thee. **Amen.**

O Lord our God, who hast bidden the light to shine out of darkness, and hast wakened us again to praise thy goodness and ask for thy grace: accept now, in thy endless mercy, the sacrifice of our worship and thanksgiving. Make us to be children of the light and of the day, and heirs of thine everlasting inheritance. Pour out upon us the riches of thy mercy, so that we, redeemed in soul and body, and steadfast in faith, may ever praise thy wonderful and holy name; through Jesus Christ our Lord. **Amen.**

**End of Year**

O eternal and almighty God, who hast been the dwelling-place of thy people in all generations, whose mercies are more than we can number, and whose compassions are without end: grant us, we beseech thee, the help of thy Holy Spirit, that we may worthily praise thee for thine untold goodness, and give ourselves anew to thee for thy service and glory; through Jesus Christ our Lord. **Amen.**

**New Year**

Almighty God, who art, and wast, and art to come, who rulest over all and makest all things new; and who in thy providence and love hast brought us to the beginning of another year; grant that in our worship we may proclaim the wonders of thy grace, and make thy praise glorious: for to thee, Father, Son, and Holy Spirit, we ascribe all honour, majesty, and dominion, for ever and ever. **Amen.**

**Sundays Before Easter**

Almighty God, eternal Father, who didst not spare thine own Son, but didst deliver him up for us all: in humility and penitence we draw nigh unto thee. As we call to remembrance the passion and sufferings of thy holy Son, we beseech thee to stir up within us the precious gift of faith, that we may rejoice in thy great salvation, and offer unto thee the worship of our hearts and the obedience of our lives; through the same Jesus Christ our Lord. **Amen.**

O Lord, our God, who hast called us to prayer: stir our hearts with the thought of thy goodness, and grant us the spirit of true devotion, that we may worthily praise him who suffered and went down to death, that he might open to us the gates of eternal life, even Jesus Christ our Lord. **Amen.**

### Palm Sunday

O merciful Father, who by the passion and death of Jesus Christ thy Son hast redeemed us all: hear us as we praise thee for the wonder of thy love, the riches of thy grace, and the glory of thy salvation; and so renew our hearts by thy Holy Spirit that may know thy peace and glorify thy name; through Jesus Christ our Lord. **Amen.**

### Easter

O God, thou art our God, we praise thee: thou art our God, we exalt thee. Blessed be thy glorious name that thou didst not suffer thine Holy One to see corruption, but didst raise him up in triumph over death. Grant us thy grace, O God, that we may give thanks to thee, who hast given us the victory through our Lord Jesus Christ; to whom be glory for ever and ever. **Amen.**

### Sundays After Easter

O living God, awaken us, we pray thee, to thy presence, that we may know the power of that endless life which thou dost give to us thy children; through Jesus Christ our Lord. **Amen.**

**Day of Pentecost**

Come, thou Holy Spirit:
restore the lives which, without thee, are as dead;
kindle the hearts which, without thee, are cold and
dull; enlighten the minds which, without thee, are
dark and blind; fill the church which, without thee,
is an empty shrine; and teach us how to pray.
**Amen.**

*Minister.*

People ought always to praise you.
God of earth and heaven.

*People.*

All of us ought to praise you.
You are always there, never growing old,
    fresh as each new day.
You were in Jesus,
    showing us your love by his death;
    and, by his resurrection,
    giving us hope of living with you for ever.
You bring life and light to the world by your
    Holy Spirit,
    making every moment your moment,
    and every day your day of coming to the rescue.

*Minister and People.*

To God the Father, God the Son, God the Holy
    Spirit,
Let all the world give praise,
    today and every day,
    and for ever and ever. **Amen.**

O almighty God, who on the day of Pentecost didst fulfil thy promise, given through the prophets and renewed by Jesus Christ, to send the Holy Spirit upon thy church: grant that he may come upon us this day, to shed abroad thy love in our hearts, to take of the things of Christ and show them unto us, and to enable us to worship thee in spirit and in truth; through Jesus Christ our Lord. **Amen.**

### Sundays After Pentecost

Glory be to thee, O God the Father almighty, Maker of heaven and earth, of whose faithfulness there is no end. Glory be to thee, O Lord Jesus Christ, the Saviour of the world, who by thy Cross and precious blood hast redeemed us. Glory be to thee, O God the Holy Spirit, the Lord and Giver of life, who dost take of the things of Christ and show them unto us. O holy and eternal God, Father, Son and Holy Spirit, to thee we ascribe all blessing and honour and glory, now and for ever. **Amen.**

God the Father, God beyond us, we adore you.
    You are the depth of all that is.
    You are the ground of our being.

God the Son, God beside us, we adore you.
    You are the perfection of humanity.
    You have shown us what human life should be like.

God the Spirit, God around us, we adore you.
    You are the power within us.
    You can make us the men and women we are meant to be.

Father, Son, and Spirit;
God, beyond, beside and around us;
We adore you. **Amen.**

Almighty God, our heavenly Father, in whom alone our hearts find rest and peace; reveal thyself to us in this hour of worship, pour down upon us thy spiritual gifts, and grant that we may be refreshed and strengthened to finish the work which thou hast given us to do; through Jesus Christ our Lord. **Amen.**

Eternal God, most blessed and most holy, we worship and adore thee. We acknowledge thine infinite glory, we celebrate thy divine majesty, we praise thee for the wonder of thy love in Jesus Christ our Lord. Accept, we pray thee, the adoration of our hearts, and by thy Holy Spirit enable us to worship thee in the beauty of holiness; for to thee, Father, Son and Holy Spirit, we ascribe all honour and glory, now and for ever. **Amen.**

Great and marvellous are thy works, Lord God almighty; just and true are thy ways, thou King of saints. Who shall not fear thee, O Lord, and glorify thy name? for thou only art holy. Wherefore with thy whole Church in heaven and on earth we worship and adore thee, Father, Son, and Holy Spirit; to whom be glory for ever and ever. **Amen.**

Almighty God, our heavenly Father, in whom alone the heart of man finds peace: draw near to us in this time of worship, that, being cleansed and strengthened by thy Spirit, we may serve thee with a quiet mind. **Amen.**

Almighty God, most blessed and most holy, before the brightness of whose presence the angels veil their faces: with lowly reverence and adoring love we acknowledge thine infinite glory, and worship thee, Father, Son, and Holy Spirit, eternal Trinity. Blessing, and honour, and glory, and power be unto our God, for ever and ever. **Amen.**

Almighty God, our heavenly Father, who reignest over all things in thy wisdom, power, and love; we humble ourselves in thy presence, adoring thee for thy glory and majesty, and praising thee for thy grace and truth revealed to us in thy Son our Saviour. Grant us the help of thy Holy Spirit, that we may worship thee in spirit and in truth; through Jesus Christ our Lord. **Amen.**

### General

Almighty God, our heavenly Father, who dost ever meet with thy people to bless them: make us joyful in thy house of prayer, and grant that our worship, being offered in the name and in the spirit of thy Son, may be acceptable unto thee; through the same Jesus Christ our Lord. **Amen.**

O God of truth, who art worthy of nobler praises than we can offer and of purer worship than we can imagine, assist us in our prayers and draw us to thyself, that what is lacking in our words and thoughts may be supplied by thy overflowing love; through Jesus Christ our Lord. **Amen.**

Almighty God, from whom every good prayer cometh: deliver us, when we draw near to thee, from coldness of heart and wanderings of mind, that with steadfast thought and kindled desire we may worship thee in the faith and spirit of Jesus Christ our Lord. **Amen.**

Almighty God, unto whom all hearts be open, all desires known, and from whom no secrets are hid: cleanse the thoughts of our hearts by the inspiration of thy Holy Spirit, that we may perfectly love thee, and worthily magnify thy holy name; through Christ our Lord. **Amen.**

Almighty God, our heavenly Father, you have made us for yourself and called us into your fellowship. Grant that today, while we worship you here, we may receive your blessing and may be equipped by your Spirit to witness to you throughout another week; through Jesus Christ our Lord. **Amen.**

## 3. CONFESSIONS OF SIN

Almighty and most merciful Father, we have erred and strayed from thy ways like lost sheep, we have followed too much the devices and desires of our own hearts, we have offended against thy holy laws, we have left undone those things which we ought to have done, and we have done those things which we ought not to have done, and there is no health in us. But thou, O Lord, have mercy upon us. Spare thou them, O God, which confess their faults. Restore thou them that are penitent, according to thy promises declared unto mankind in Christ Jesus our Lord. And grant, O most merciful Father, for his sake, that we may hereafter live a godly, righteous, and sober life, to the glory of thy holy Name. **Amen.**

Most holy and merciful Father, we acknowledge and confess in thy presence, our sinful nature prone to evil and slothful in good, and all our shortcomings and offences against thee. Thou alone knowest how often we have sinned, in wandering from thy ways, in wasting thy gifts, in forgetting thy love. But thou, O Lord, have pity upon us, who are ashamed and sorry for all wherein we have displeased thee. Teach us to hate our errors, cleanse us from our secret faults, and forgive our sins, for the sake of thy dear Son our Saviour. And O most holy and loving Father, send thy purifying grace into our hearts, we beseech thee, that we may henceforth live in thy light and walk in thy ways, according to the commandments of Jesus Christ our Lord. **Amen.**

O God, we confess
> our failure to be true even to our own accepted standards;
> our choosing of the worse when we know the better;
> our unwillingness to apply to ourselves the standards of conduct we demand of others;
> our complacence towards wrongs that do not touch our own case and our oversensitiveness to those that do;
> our slowness to see the good in our fellows and to see the evil in ourselves;

our hardness of heart towards our neighbours'
faults and our readiness to make allowances
for our own;
O Lord, forgive. **Amen.**


O merciful God, whose judgement is altogether
true and righteous, we confess before thee the sin
which does so easily beset us:
our indolence and sloth in our work;
our stubborn adherence to prejudice, evading
the pain of growth;
our scorn of old ways because they are old, and
indulgence in new follies to prove ourselves
modern;
our self-pity under sacrifice, and easy justifica-
tion of our failures;
our rebellion against the discipline of thought,
prayer and life by which thou wouldst fit us
for service in thy church;
our secret shame which we acknowledge before
thee in the silence of our private confession.
**Amen.**

O God,
We confess that thy church has often been deaf
to thy voice.
We confess that it has been busied with things
of little worth, concerned more for its own
comfort than for carrying the cross.
We confess that its unity has been shattered by
divisions, and that the factious spirit has often
replaced the spirit of peace and brotherhood.

We confess that, though we have known the call of God to the church, we have been slow and unadventurous in answering it.

We confess that we do not exhibit the witness of Christian life and love.

We confess that we have failed to use those mighty powers with which our Saviour has promised to endow his church. **Amen.**

Eternal God, our judge and redeemer: we confess that we have tried to hide from thee, for we have done wrong. We have lived for ourselves. We have refused to shoulder the troubles of others, and turned from our neighbours. We have ignored the pain of the world, and passed by the hungry, the poor, and the oppressed. O God, in thy great mercy, forgive our sin and free us from selfishness, that we may choose thy will and obey thy commandments; through Jesus Christ our Lord. **Amen.**

O God, we confess
the things we try to hide from you,
the things we try to hide from others,
the things we try to hide from ourselves.
We confess
the heartbreak, worry, and sorrow we have caused, and that make it hard for others to forgive us;
the times we have made it easy for others to go wrong;
the harm we have done, and cannot undo, and that make it hard for us to forgive ourselves.
Lord have mercy and forgive us. **Amen.**

O God, we confess
    the blindness that is not even aware of sinning;
    the pride that dares not admit that it is wrong;
    the self that can see nothing but its own will;
    the righteousness that knows no fault;
    the callousness that has ceased to care;
    the defiance that does not regret its own sins;
    the evasion that always tries to make excuses;
    the heart that is too hardened to repent.
Grant, O Lord, that we may be forgiven; through
    Jesus Christ our Lord. **Amen.**

*Minister.*

Let us confess to our God our sins as members of
    this congregation.
For coming into thy presence with unclean lips
    and impure hearts, O Lord:

*People.*
Forgive us, we pray thee.

*Minister.*

For bringing jealousies and resentments into our
    life as a congregation, O Lord:

*People.*
Forgive us, we pray thee.

*Minister.*

For wasting time we have set aside for thy service,
    O Lord:

*People.*
Forgive us, we pray thee.

*Minister.*

For accepting help from others without giving, and for offering help to others in the hope of receiving, O Lord:

*People.*

Forgive us, we pray thee.

*Minister.*

For praising thee here more fervently than in our daily living, O Lord:

*People.*

Forgive us, we pray thee.

*Minister.*

For every unchristlike attitude that corrupts our worship and weakens our witness, O Lord:

*People.*

Forgive us, we pray thee.

*Minister.*

Accept us and use us in thy service, we ask thee in Christ's name. **Amen.**

Loving Father, who dost look with mercy upon thy servants: we enter this thy house of worship with lives tainted by failure and deliberate transgression. When challenged to go out in service, we have closed our ears and turned away. When confronted with temptation's allure, we have easily given in. In our daily lives we have been irritable and resentful and rude. Above all, O God, we have presumed to be more righteous than we are. Forgive, we pray, and consecrate us anew for thy service, that we may go forth in the assurance of thy love and the confidence of thy power; through Christ our Lord. **Amen.**

O Lord, who alone can purify the heart of man:
   we confess that we are
   prone to ease and pleasure,
   averse to self-discipline and sacrifice,
   anxious to hear something new, yet indifferent
     to the good news of Christ,
   zealous in getting, cautious in giving,
   eager in amusement, slothful in service,
   sudden in anger, slow to forgive,
   ready to promise, reluctant to perform.
O Lord, have mercy upon us. **Amen.**

We confess, O God, that we have sinned against you, against ourselves, and against our neighbours. We have called on your name, but we have not done your will for us. We have esteemed ourselves, but we have not respected your image in us. We have sought the company of others, but not always their good. Forgive us, we pray, and make us what you desire us to be; through Jesus Christ our Lord. **Amen.**

Most holy and merciful Father, we acknowledge and confess in your presence the smallness of our love, the narrowness of our concern, the obstinate rejection of our true humanity. Through our careless hands have slipped opportunities not taken, people not cared for, days not celebrated. Have pity upon us, Lord, who are ashamed and sorry for the ways of our disobedience. **Amen.**

We confess to you God that we have sinned in
    what we have thought, said and done.
We confess that we have sinned also in what we
    have not thought, or said, or done.
Before all your people we confess this to you,
    we confess it openly to one another.
These our faults have hurt us and hurt others;
    we cannot stand them any longer.
      Help us.
      Rid us of our guilt. **Amen.**

## 4. ASSURANCE OF PARDON

Now let us be comforted and be glad, and hear
the good tidings of the gospel: God so loved the
world that he gave his only Son, that whoever
believes in him should not perish but have eternal
life.

Let us receive the promise of grace and the assurance of pardon given to all who believe and repent: This is a faithful saying, and worthy of all
acceptance, that Christ Jesus came into the world
to save sinners.
Praise be to God.

Hear these words addressed to penitent believers:
If any one does sin, we have an advocate with the
Father, Jesus Christ the righteous; and he is the
expiation for our sins, and not for ours only but
also for the sins of the whole world.
Be assured, then, that God has forgiven your sins.

Hear the good news of the gospel:

The conclusion of the matter is this,

There is now no condemnation for those who are united with Christ Jesus, because in Christ Jesus the life-giving law of the Spirit has set you free from the law of sin and death.

Be assured, then, that God grants you pardon for your sins.

God has exalted Jesus Christ with his own right hand, as leader and saviour, to grant repentance and forgiveness of sins.

Therefore, all those, who as servants of Jesus Christ believe and repent, are assured of God's pardon and forgiveness.

In Christ our release is secured and our sins are forgiven through the shedding of his blood. Therein lies the richness of God's free grace lavished upon us.

This is our faith. This is our hope. Trusting in this grace, be assured that your sins are forgiven.

The Son of Man has come to seek and save what is lost.

Everyone who trusts in him receives forgiveness of sins through his name.

Therefore, be assured that God bestows upon you his mercy and grants you forgiveness of your sins, and leads you into life eternal.

Hear this which is proclaimed in scripture:

God was in Christ reconciling the world to himself, not counting their trespasses against them. So it is that you can be assured that your sins are forgiven.

Here is good news for you:

Christ Jesus came into the world to save sinners. If we confess our sins, God is just, and may be trusted to forgive our sins and cleanse us from every kind of wrong.
So it is that you may be assured that your sins are forgiven.

## 5. PRAYERS FOR GRACE

### Season of Creation

Most glorious Lord God, who hast created the world and upholdest its fabric in a marvellous order and beauty: give us grace so to meditate on thy workmanship and wisdom, thy power and great mercies, that we may thank thee, adore thee and praise thee for ever; through Jesus Christ our Lord. **Amen.**

O heavenly Father, who hast filled the world with beauty: open our eyes to behold thy gracious hand in all thy works, that, rejoicing in thy whole creation, we may learn to serve thee with gladness; for the sake of him by whom all things were made, thy Son Jesus Christ our Lord. **Amen.**

God our Father, who hast created us in thine own image, with a mind to understand thy works, a heart to love thee, and a will to serve thee: increase in us that knowledge, that love, and that obedience, that we may grow daily in thy likeness; through Jesus Christ our Lord. **Amen.**

O thou in whom we live and move and have our being, awaken us to thy presence that we may walk in thy world as thy children. Grant us reverence for all thy creation, that we may treat our fellow men with courtesy, and all living things with gentleness; through Jesus Christ our Lord. **Amen.**

Almighty God, whose glory the heavens are telling, who art the breath of life of all things living: to thee be praise from all thy creatures, and from man, made in thine own image, redeemed and restored by Jesus Christ thine only Son, our Lord. **Amen.**

O God, who hast made all things, the flowers and trees and the green grass, the sea, the sky, the stars, the birds, and all living things: and hast made man in thine own image, that he might know who is the creator of all these things; open our eyes to see thee everywhere and glorify thee in thy works; through Jesus Christ our Lord. **Amen.**

Almighty God, you have given us authority to rule the earth according to your will: enable us to manage things with reason and love, that the whole creation may give you praise; through Jesus Christ our Lord. **Amen.**

Almighty God and heavenly Father, whose Son Jesus Christ shared in Nazareth the life of an earthly home: send down thy blessings, we pray thee, upon all Christian families, that parents by the spirit of understanding and wisdom, and children by the spirit of obedience and reverence, may be bound each to each by mutual love; through him who became a child, and learned obedience to thy will, even Jesus Christ our Lord. **Amen.**

### World-wide Communion Sunday

Almighty God, who hast manifested thy Son Jesus Christ to be a light to mankind: grant that we thy people, being nourished by thy word and sacraments, may be strengthened to show forth to all men the unsearchable riches of Christ, so that he may be known, adored, and obeyed, to the ends of the earth; who liveth and reigneth with thee and the Holy Spirit, one God, world without end. **Amen.**

O Lord Jesus Christ, who hast ordained the signs whereby we are assured of thy gracious work in us: grant that, being born anew of water and the Spirit, we may by faith receive thy precious body and blood, and, in union with thee, offer ourselves a living sacrifice, holy and acceptable to the Father; who liveth and reigneth with thee and the Holy Spirit, ever one God, world without end. **Amen.**

### Sunday Before Thanksgiving Day

Almighty and everlasting God, who dost graciously give us the fruits of the earth in their season: we offer thee humble and hearty thanks for these thy bounties, beseeching thee to give us grace rightly to use them to thy glory and for the relief of those in need; through Jesus Christ our Lord. **Amen.**

Lord Jesus, who for our sake didst become poor, that by thy poverty we might become rich: grant to thy people so to give of their substance as to acknowledge that they belong wholly to thee; for thine own sake. **Amen.**

### Remembrance Sunday

Almighty God, who art our refuge and our strength, we humble ourselves in thy presence, and, as we make solemn remembrance before thee this day of the great things that have been done for us, we earnestly seek thy mercy and thy grace; through Jesus Christ our Lord. **Amen.**

### All Saints' Day

O almighty God, who hast knit together thine elect in one communion and fellowship, in the mystical body of thy Son Christ our Lord: grant us grace so to follow thy blessed saints in all virtuous and godly living, that we may come to those unspeakable joys, which thou hast prepared for them that unfeignedly love thee; through Jesus Christ our Lord. **Amen.**

### Sundays Before Christmas

O Lord Jesus Christ, who at thy first coming didst send thy messenger to prepare thy way before thee: grant that we, paying urgent heed to the message of repentance, may with hearts prepared await thy final coming to judge the world; who with the Father and the Holy Spirit ever livest and reignest, one God, world without end. **Amen.**

Make us, we pray thee, O Lord our God, watchful in awaiting the coming of thy Son, Christ our Lord; that when he shall come and knock, he may find us not sleeping in sin, but awake and rejoicing in his praises; through the same Jesus Christ our Lord. **Amen.**

O God, whose throne is set eternal in the heavens: make ready for thy gracious rule the kingdoms of this world; come with haste, and save us; that violence and crying may be no more, and righteousness and peace may bless thy children; through Jesus Christ our Lord, who lives and reigns with thee and the Holy Spirit, ever one God. **Amen.**

Almighty God, give us grace that we may cast away the works of darkness, and put upon us the armour of light, now in the time of this mortal life, in which thy Son Jesus Christ came to visit us in great humility; that in the last day, when he shall come again in his glorious majesty to judge both the quick and the dead, we may rise to the life immortal; through him who liveth and reigneth with thee and the Holy Spirit, now and ever. **Amen.**

### Christmas Eve

Grant us, O God, such love and wonder, that with humble shepherds, wise men, and pilgrims unknown, we may come and adore the holy Child, the heavenly King; and with our gifts worship and serve him, our Lord and Saviour, Jesus Christ. **Amen.**

Holy Father, who brought to earth peace and good-will in the birth of thy Son Jesus: fill us with such gladness, that like the shepherds and wise men, we may come to worship him who is Lord of Lords and King of Kings, Jesus Christ our Saviour. **Amen.**

### Christmas Day

O God, who makest us glad with the yearly re-membrance of the birth of thy Son Jesus Christ: grant that as we joyfully receive him for our Re-deemer, so we may with sure confidence behold him when he shall come to be our Judge; who liveth and reigneth with thee and the Holy Spirit, one God, world without end. **Amen.**

O God, who before all others didst call shepherds to the cradle of thy Son: grant that by the preach-ing of the gospel the poor, the humble, and the forgotten, may know that they are at home with thee; through Jesus Christ our Lord. **Amen.**

Glory be to thee, O God in the highest, who by the birth of thy beloved Son hast made him to be for us both word and sacrament: grant that we may hear thy word, receive thy grace, and be made one with him born for our salvation; even Jesus Christ the Lord. **Amen.**

Sundays After Christmas

Almighty God, the giver of strength and joy: change, we pray thee, our bondage into liberty, and the poverty of our nature into the riches of thy grace; that by the transformation of our lives glory may be revealed; through Jesus Christ, our Lord. **Amen.**

Almighty and everlasting God, who art always more ready to hear than we to pray, and art wont to give more than either we desire, or deserve: pour down upon us the abundance of thy mercy, forgiving us those things whereof our conscience is afraid, and giving us those good things which we are not worthy to ask, but through the merits and mediation of Jesus Christ, thy Son, our Lord. **Amen.**

O God, who knowest us to be in the midst of so many dangers, that we cannot always stand upright: grant to us such strength and protection that we may be supported in all difficulty, and our feet be set against temptation; through Jesus Christ our Lord. **Amen.**

O God, you have summoned us to be doers of the word: grant us strength to fulfil your commandments; to do justly, to love mercy, and to walk humbly with you; through Jesus Christ our Lord. **Amen.**

New Year

Eternal God, in whose sight a thousand years are as an evening past: as you have led us in days gone by, so guide us now and always, that our hearts may turn to seek your will and our resolves be strengthened; through Jesus Christ our Lord. **Amen.**

### Epiphany

O God, who by a star didst guide the wise men to the worship of thy Son: lead, we pray thee, to thyself the wise and the great in every land, that unto thee every knee may bow, and every thought be brought into captivity; through Jesus Christ our Lord. **Amen.**

O God, who by the leading of a star revealed thy newborn Son to those afar off: mercifully grant that we who know thee by faith, may in this life glorify thee, and in the life to come behold thee face to face; through the same thy Son, Jesus Christ our Lord. **Amen.**

O Lord Jesus Christ, who didst humble thyself to take the baptism of sinful men, and wast forthwith declared to be the Son of God: grant that we who have been baptized into thee may rejoice to be the sons of God, and servants of all; for thy name's sake, who with the Father and the Holy Spirit livest and reignest ever one God, world without end. **Amen.**

### Week of Prayer for Christian Unity

O God, the Creator and Father of all mankind, who by thy Holy Spirit hast made a diversity of peoples one in the confession of thy name: lead them, we pray thee, by the same Spirit to display to the whole earth one mind in belief and one passion for righteousness; through Jesus Christ our Lord. **Amen.**

**Sundays Before Easter**

Almighty and everlasting God, who hatest nothing that thou hast made, and dost forgive the sins of all those who are penitent: create and make in us new and contrite hearts, that we, worthily lamenting our sins and acknowledging our wretchedness, may obtain of thee, the God of all mercy, perfect remission and forgiveness; through Jesus Christ our Lord. **Amen.**

O Lord, who for our sake didst fast forty days and forty nights: give us grace to use such abstinence, that, our flesh being subdued to the spirit, we may ever obey thy godly motions in righteousness, and true holiness, to thy honour and glory; who livest and reignest with the Father and the Holy Spirit, one God, world without end. **Amen.**

Almighty God, who givest us our quiet seasons of thought and prayer: help us now and at all times to find in thee our true peace. Save us in the hour of trial; deliver us from evil thoughts and desires, and from the tyranny of outward things. May we learn of Christ to be strong and brave in the struggle with temptation, and to overcome even as he overcame. **Amen.**

O Lord, we beseech thee favourably to hear the prayers of thy people; that we, who are justly afflicted for our offences, may be mercifully delivered by thy goodness, for the glory of thy name; through Jesus Christ our Saviour, who liveth and reigneth with thee and the Holy Spirit, ever one God, world without end. **Amen.**

O God, we are prone to bring back the troubles of yesterday, and to forecast the cares of tomorrow; give us grace to throw off our fears and anxieties, as our Lord has commanded; that, this and every day, we may be kept in your peace; through Jesus Christ our Lord. **Amen.**

O Lord Jesus, you set your face steadfastly to go to Jerusalem; deliver us from timid minds that shrink from the harder paths of duty; and prepare us to welcome your command to take up our cross and follow you, who are the author and finisher of our faith. **Amen.**

O blessed Saviour, who by thy cross and passion didst give life to the world: we pray thee to enlighten, visit, and comfort all thy servants who bear the cross and glory in thy name; whom with the Father and the Holy Spirit we worship and glorify, one God, for ever and ever. **Amen.**

### Palm Sunday

O Christ, the King of glory, who didst enter the holy city in meekness to be made perfect through the suffering of death: give us grace, we pray thee, in all our life here to take up our cross daily and follow thee, that hereafter we may rejoice with thee in thy heavenly kingdom; who livest and reignest with the Father and the Holy Spirit, God, world without end. **Amen.**

### Maundy Thursday

Be present, O Lord, unto us, we beseech thee, and as thou gavest us an example by washing the feet

of thy disciples and wiping them free from all outward defilement, so grant us grace ever to serve
one another in true humility, and do thou vouchsafe that we may have the inward defilement of all
our sins made clean by thee; who livest and reignest with the Father in the unity of the Holy Spirit,
one God, world without end. **Amen.**

O Lord Jesus Christ, who hast ordained this holy
sacrament to be a pledge of thy love, and a continual remembrance of thy death and resurrection:
grant that we, who partake thereof by faith with
thanksgiving, may grow up into thee in all things,
until we come to thy eternal joy; who with the
Father and the Holy Spirit livest and reignest, one
God, world without end. **Amen.**

### Good Friday

Almighty God, we beseech thee graciously to behold this thy family, for which our Lord Jesus Christ
was content to be betrayed, and given up into the
hands of wicked men, and to suffer death upon the
cross; who now liveth and reigneth with thee and
the Holy Spirit, ever one God, world without end.
**Amen.**

O Saviour of the world, who by thy cross and
precious blood hast redeemed us: save us, and
help us, we humbly beseech thee, O Lord. **Amen.**

### Easter Day

O God, who by thine only-begotten Son hast overcome death and opened to us the gate of everlasting life: grant that we who celebrate the fes-
tival of our Lord's resurrection may by the renew-

ing of thy Spirit arise from the death of the soul; through Jesus Christ our Lord. **Amen.**

O God, who through the mighty resurrection of thy Son Jesus Christ from the dead hast delivered us from the power of darkness into the kingdom of thy love: grant, we beseech thee, that as by his death he has recalled us into life, so by his presence ever abiding in us he may raise us to joys eternal; through him who for our sakes died and rose again, and is ever with us in power and great glory, even the same Jesus Christ our Lord. **Amen.**

### Sundays After Easter

Grant, O God, that we who have celebrated the resurrection of Jesus Christ from the dead may demonstrate his victory in our daily conduct and face the future unafraid; through the same Jesus Christ our Lord. **Amen.**

O God, who for our redemption didst give thine only-begotten Son to the death of the Cross, and by his glorious resurrection hast delivered us from the power of our enemy: grant us so to die daily unto sin, that we may evermore live with him in the joy of his resurrection; through the same Jesus Christ our Lord. **Amen.**

O thou who art the Light of the minds that know thee, the Life of the souls that love thee, and the Strength of the wills that serve thee: help us so to know thee that we may truly love thee, so to love thee that we may fully serve thee, whose service is perfect freedom; through Jesus Christ our Lord. **Amen.**

Lord Jesus, good Shepherd of the sheep, who came to seek and save the lost: so lead your church that we may show your compassion to the helpless, rescue those in peril, and bring home the wanderers in safety to you. **Amen.**

Mighty God, whose Son Jesus broke the bonds of death and scattered the powers of darkness: arm us with such faith in him that that we may face both death and evil, and overcome even as he overcame; in your name. **Amen.**

O Lord Jesus Christ, who art the Way, the Truth, and the Life: allow us not, we pray thee, to wander from thee, who art the Way; nor to distrust thee, who art the Truth; nor to look for strength anywhere but in thee, who art the Life; ever living and reigning with the Father and the Holy Spirit, one God, world without end. **Amen.**

### Sunday Before Ascension Day

Almighty God, grant that, as our Lord Jesus Christ ascended into heaven, we may also in heart and mind be lifted up and continually dwell with him who lives and reigns with thee and the Holy Spirit, one God, forever. **Amen.**

### Sunday After Ascension Day

O God, the King of glory, who hast exalted thine only Son Jesus Christ with great triumph unto thy kingdom in heaven: we pray thee, leave us not comfortless, but send to us thy Holy Spirit to comfort us, and exalt us unto the same place whither our Saviour Christ is gone before, who liveth and reigneth with thee and the Holy Spirit, one God, world without end. **Amen.**

### Pentecost

O God, who in the exaltation of thy Son Jesus Christ dost sanctify thy universal church: shed abroad in every race and nation the gift of his Spirit; that the work wrought by his power at the first preaching of the gospel may be extended throughout the whole world; through the same our Lord Jesus Christ, who liveth and reigneth with thee in the unity of the same Spirit now and ever. **Amen.**

O thou who sent the promised fire of thy Spirit to make saints of ordinary men: grant that we, waiting and together now, may be inflamed with such love for thee that we may speak out boldly in thy name; through Jesus Christ our Lord. **Amen.**

### Sundays After Pentecost

Startle us, O God, with your truth, and open our minds to your Spirit, that this day we may receive you humbly and find hope fulfilled in Christ Jesus our Lord. **Amen.**

O Lord, who hast taught us that all our doings without charity are nothing worth: send thy Holy Spirit, and pour into our hearts that most excellent gift of charity, the very bond of peace and of all virtues, without which whosoever liveth is counted dead before thee; grant this for thine only Son Jesus Christ's sake. **Amen.**

Almighty God, you have commanded us to love our enemies and to do good to those who hate us: grant that we may not be content with the affections of our friends but may reach out in love to all thy children; through Jesus Christ our Lord.

**Amen.**

Eternal God, you have taught us that we shall live if we love you and our neighbour; help us to know who is our neighbor and to serve him, that we may truly love you; through Jesus Christ our Lord.

**Amen.**

Lord of all power and might, who art the author and giver of all good things: graft in our hearts the love of thy name, increase in us true religion, nourish us with all goodness, and of thy great mercy keep us in the same; through Jesus Christ our Lord. **Amen.**

O Lord, who hast promised that thy joy would be in us, so that our joy might be full: grant that, living close to thee, we may learn to rejoice and give thanks in all things; for thy loving mercy's sake. **Amen.**

O God, who hast prepared for them that love thee such good things as pass man's understanding: pour into our hearts such love towards thee, that we, loving thee above all things, may obtain thy promises, which exceed all that we can desire; through Jesus Christ our Lord. **Amen.**

Look graciously upon us, O Holy Spirit, and give us for our hallowing thoughts that pass into prayer, prayers that pass into love, and love that passeth into life with thee for ever. **Amen.**

Let thy merciful ears, O Lord, be open to the prayers of thy humble servants; and that they may obtain their petitions make them to ask such things as shall please thee; through Jesus Christ our Lord.

**Amen.**

O God, forasmuch as without thee we are not able to please thee; mercifully grant, that thy Holy Spirit may in all things direct and rule our hearts; through Jesus Christ our Lord. **Amen.**

O God the Redeemer, who didst send thy servant Moses to lead thy people out of bondage and affliction: Give to us and to all nations leaders obedient to thee, to teach us to know and to keep thy laws, and to bring us on our way to that country which thou hast prepared for us; through Jesus Christ our Lord. **Amen.**

**The Inauguration of
the United Church of Canada (June 10th)**

O God, who to an expectant and united church didst grant at Pentecost the gift of the Holy Spirit, and hast wonderfully brought into one fold those who now worship thee here: grant us the help of the same Spirit in all our life and worship, that we may expect great things from thee, and attempt great things for thee, and being one in thee may show to the world that thou didst send Jesus Christ our Lord, to whom, with thee and the Holy Spirit, be all honour and glory, world without end. **Amen.**

### Sunday Before Dominion Day

O God of all nations, look in mercy, we beseech thee, on our land. Give wisdom and understanding to the Queen, the Prime Minister, and all her rulers, and to her people unity and concord. Guide their policies by the light of thy life-giving Spirit, that she may go forward in justice and liberty, prosperity and peace; and in thy good time grant that she may bring her glory and honour into the kingdom of thy blessed Son, Jesus Christ our Lord. **Amen.**

O God, who art the Ruler and the Judge of all nations, look mercifully on our land. Sanctify all that is rich and noble in our traditions. Grant that our ideals and aspirations may be in accordance with thy will. Give us humility in our relations with others and sobriety in our dealings at home. Help us to discipline ourselves so that our national freedom may be used for the common good, and may bring us all to the knowledge of him whose service is perfect freedom, even Jesus Christ our Lord and Saviour. **Amen.**

### Labour Sunday

O God, who movest in love unceasing, and dost give to each man his appointed work: help us steadfastly, and as in thy sight, to fulfil the duties of our calling; that when our Lord shall take account of us, we may be found faithful in that which is least, and enter into his eternal joy. **Amen.**

## 6. PRAYERS FOR ILLUMINATION

O Lord and Lover of men, cause the pure light of thy divine knowledge to shine forth in our hearts, and open the eyes of our understanding, that we may comprehend the precepts of thy gospel; through Jesus Christ our Lord. **Amen.**

O God, the Father of light, by thy word thou hast given light unto our souls. Pour down on us the spirit of wisdom and understanding. Grant that, being taught of thee in holy Scripture, we may receive with faith the words of eternal life, and be made wise unto salvation; through Jesus Christ our Lord. **Amen.**

Let the words of our mouths and the meditations of our hearts be acceptable in thy sight, O Lord.

**Amen.**

O God, let the gospel of thy Son come to us, not in word alone, but in power. Let thy Holy Spirit teach us, so that we may receive with understanding what thou hast revealed, and eagerly do what thou hast commanded; through Jesus Christ our Lord. **Amen.**

O Lord our God, who has given thy word to be a lamp unto our feet and a light unto our path: grant us grace to receive thy truth in faith and love, that by it we may be prepared unto every good word and work, to the glory of thy name; through Jesus Christ our Lord. **Amen.**

Let the same mind be in us, our Father, which was in Christ Jesus our Lord. If we speak, let us speak the truth, and if we listen, let us listen with the will to understand and obey; in Jesus' name. **Amen.**

O God, who hast so made us that we live not by bread alone, but by every word of thine: cause us to hunger after the food of thy word, and find in it our daily need; through Jesus Christ our Lord.
**Amen.**

Almighty God, in whom are contained all the treasures of wisdom and knowledge: open our eyes that we may behold wonderful things in thy word, and give us grace to understand thy will clearly, and to choose freely the way of thy wisdom; through Jesus Christ our Lord. **Amen.**

O God, who didst command the light to shine out of darkness: shine into our hearts, to give the light of the knowledge of thy glory in the face of Jesus Christ; to whom, with thee and the Holy Spirit, be honour and praise, now and for evermore. **Amen.**

O Lord of light, make pure our hearts, that we may see thee; reveal thyself to us that we may love thee; strengthen our wills, that we may choose the good from the evil, and day by day manifest in the world the glory and the power of thy blessed gospel, which thou hast made known to us through thy Son Jesus Christ. **Amen.**

O God, whose word is sharper than any two-edged sword, piercing both heart and conscience with many wounds: let the sword of the Spirit pierce us through, and grant that the wounds that are made by thy truth may be healed by thy love; through Jesus Christ our Lord. **Amen.**

O God, whose word is quick and powerful, and sharper than any two-edged sword: grant that we may receive thy truth into our hearts, in faith and love. By it may we be taught and guided, upheld and comforted, that we be no longer children in understanding, but grow to the stature of perfect men in Christ, and be prepared unto every good word and work, to the honour of thy name; through Jesus Christ our Lord. **Amen.**

Prepare our hearts, O Lord, to accept your word. Silence in us any voice but your own, that hearing, we may also obey your will; through Jesus Christ our Lord. **Amen.**

Guide us, O Lord, by your word and Holy Spirit, that in your light we may see light, in your truth find freedom, and in your will discover your peace; through Jesus Christ our Lord. **Amen.**

## 7. ASCRIPTIONS OF GLORY

O the depth of the riches and wisdom and knowledge of God! How unsearchable are his judgments and how inscrutable his ways! For from him and through him and to him are all things. To him be glory forever. **Amen.**       *Romans 11.33 and 36*

Now to him who by the power at work within us is able to do far more abundantly than all that we ask or think, to him be glory in the church and in Christ Jesus to all generations, for ever and ever.
**Amen.**

*Ephesians 3.20*

To the King of ages, immortal, invisible, the only God, be honour and glory for ever and ever.
**Amen.**

*I Timothy 1.17*

To the blessed and only Sovereign, the King of kings and Lord of lords, who alone has immortality and dwells in unapproachable light, whom no man has ever seen or can see, to him be honour and eternal dominion. **Amen.**      *I Timothy 6.15, 16*

Now to him who is able to keep you from falling and to present you without blemish before the presence of his glory with rejoicing, to the only God, our Saviour through Jesus Christ our Lord, be glory, majesty, dominion, and authority, before all time and now and for ever. **Amen.**      *Jude 24*

To him who loves us and has freed us from our sins by his blood and made us a kingdom, priests to his God and Father, to him be glory and dominion for ever and ever. **Amen.**      *Revelation 1.5, 6*

Worthy art thou, our Lord and God,
    to receive glory and honour and power,
    for thou didst create all things,
    and by thy will they existed and were created.
**Amen.**

*Revelation 4.11*

Worthy is the Lamb who was slain, to receive power and wealth and wisdom and might and honour and glory and blessing! **Amen.**

*Revelation 5.12*

To him who sits upon the throne and to the Lamb be blessing and honour and glory and might for ever and ever. **Amen.** *Revelation 5.13*

Amen! Blessing and glory and wisdom and thanksgiving and honour and power and might be to our God for ever and ever! **Amen.** *Revelation 7.12*

Great and wonderful are thy deeds,
O Lord God the Almighty!
Just and true are thy ways,
O King of the ages!
Who shall not fear and glorify thy name, O Lord?
For thou only art holy. **Amen.** *Revelation 15.3, 4*

Unto the Father and unto the Son and unto the Holy Spirit be ascribed in the church, all honour and glory, might, majesty, dominion and blessing, now, henceforth, and forever. **Amen.**

## 8. OFFERTORY SENTENCES AND PRAYERS

Ascribe to the Lord the glory due his name;
bring an offering, and come before him!

*I Chronicles 16.29*

The earth is the Lord's and the fulness thereof, the world and those who dwell therein.

*Psalm 24.1*

Bless the Lord, O my soul;
   and all that is within me, bless his holy name;
Bless the Lord, O my soul,
   and forget not all his benefits.    *Psalm 103.1, 2*

What shall I render to the Lord
   for all this bounty to me?
I will pay my vows to the Lord
   in the presence of all his people.    *Psalm 116.12, 14*

Honour the Lord with your substance and with the
first fruits of all your produce.    *Proverbs 3.9*

Entering the house, they saw the child with Mary
his mother, and bowed to the ground in homage to
him; then they opened their treasures, and offered
him gifts.    *Matthew 2.11*

Let your light so shine before men, that they may
see your good works and give glory to your Father
who is in heaven.    *Matthew 5.16*

What does a man gain by winning the whole world
at the cost of his true self?    *Mark 8.36*

God so loved the world that he gave his only Son,
that whoever believes in him should not perish but
have eternal life.    *John 3.16*

You know how generous our Lord Jesus Christ
has been: he was rich, yet for your sake he became
poor, so that through his poverty you might become rich.    *II Corinthians 8.9*

Each person should give as he has decided for himself; there should be no reluctance, no sense of
compulsion; God loves a cheerful giver.
   *II Corinthians 9.7*

Do not neglect to do good and to share what you have, for such sacrifices are pleasing to God.

*Hebrews 13.16*

O God, who dost teach us by this act of worship that it is more blessed to give than to receive: graciously accept these our offerings and give us the right spirit both in giving and receiving: through Jesus Christ our Lord. **Amen.**

O God, author of all goodness, who hast entrusted us with material possessions and made us stewards of thy bounty: accept the offerings which now we present to thee; through Jesus Christ our Lord.

**Amen.**

Unto thee, O Lord, do we offer the gift of our hands and the loyalty of our hearts. Accept us with our gifts, we pray, in Jesus' name. **Amen.**

Almighty and merciful God, of whose generosity we have received all that we have and all that we are: grant that we may so use the things which thou hast entrusted to our care, that we ourselves may become more and more thy children in spirit and in truth; through Jesus Christ our Lord. **Amen.**

Receive, O Lord, we pray thee, these our offerings which we give for the service of thy church, and for the extension of thy kingdom; accept with them the worship of our hearts and lives; through Jesus Christ our Lord. **Amen.**

O God, the giver of every good and perfect gift, accept these offerings of thy people. Forbid that we should bring our gifts and withhold ourselves. Grant that with the tribute of our hands we may bring the consecration of our hearts. And to thee shall be the glory. **Amen.**

O God, who needest not to be enriched with any gifts that we may bring, yet who lovest the cheerful giver: receive these our offerings which we present before thee, and with them ourselves, our souls and our bodies, a living sacrifice, holy and acceptable to thee; through Jesus Christ our Lord. **Amen.**

Send down upon us, O God, thy Holy Spirit, to cleanse our hearts, to hallow our gifts, and to perfect the offering of ourselves to thee; through Jesus Christ our Lord. **Amen.**

Lord Jesus Christ, you were rich, yet for our sake you became poor, so that through your poverty we might become rich. Accept this offering as a token of our gratitude for all you have done. **Amen.**

#### At the Lord's Supper

Lord God,
> we bring to you the ordinary things of life —
>> food and drink and money —
> and in bringing them we bring ourselves.

Take us and our gifts of money
> to do your work in the world.

Take this food and drink
> from our tables to your table
> and feed us with your love.

Through Jesus Christ our Lord. **Amen.**

## 9. THANKSGIVINGS

Almighty God, Father of all mercies, we thine unworthy servants do give thee most humble and hearty thanks for all thy goodness and loving kindness to us and to all men. We bless thee for our creation, preservation, and all the blessings of this life, but above all, for thine inestimable love in the redemption of the world by our Lord Jesus Christ, for the means of grace, and for the hope of glory. And, we beseech thee, give us that due sense of all thy mercies, that our hearts may be unfeignedly thankful, and that we show forth thy praise, not only with our lips, but in our lives, by giving up ourselves to thy service, and by walking before thee in holiness and righteousness all our days; through Jesus Christ our Lord, to whom with thee and the Holy Spirit be all honour and glory, world without end. **Amen.**

Almighty God, our most gracious Father in heaven, we thank thee for thy mercies which are beyond telling.
We bless thee for the order and beauty of all that thou hast made: for the wonder of the world about us, for day and night, for summer and winter, for sun and rain, for seed-time and harvest, and for thy bountiful supply of all our needs.
We bless thee for thy goodness to us throughout the days of our earthly life: for protecting us in our weakness, for increasing and renewing our strength, for fitting us for the conflict with evil and

sin, and for calling us into thy service and into the knowledge of thy truth.

We bless thee for all whom thou hast given to be near and dear to us: for the members of our families, for our friends and comrades, for our pastors and teachers, and for all with whom we are joined in the covenant of thy church.

We bless thee, most of all, for sending thy Son to be our Saviour: for his taking of our nature, for his life on earth, for his sufferings and death, for his resurrection and reign, for his continued intercession for us, and for his gift of the Holy Spirit.

Grant, O God, that our hearts may grow in thankfulness for thy mercies, and enable us, by thy grace, to give all that we have and are for thy service, to the glory of thy name; through Jesus Christ our Lord. **Amen.**

O Lord our God, we thank you for creating the world and for preserving it until now.

We thank you for the regular return of day and night, and of the seasons,
and for the dependability of nature and of time.

We thank you for memory, which enables us to build on the experience of the past;
for imagination, which admits us to a wider world than we could otherwise know;
and for foresight, by which we plan for the future.

We thank you for your patience with the errors and sins of mankind:

you have neither wearied of us nor allowed us
    to ruin ourselves in self-destruction or utter
    degradation,
but have sent your Son Jesus Christ to break
    down the barriers between us and you and
    between us and each other,
    and to restore the broken unity of human life.
To you, O Lord, be glory forever. **Amen.**

O Lord, we thank you for your goodness to us: for
    the world which you have made and for the
    strength to serve you in it,
for disclosures of yourself, in nature, art and in the
    lives of men,
for all writings which display your truth,
for the tasks to which you are calling us,
    and for the Bible, through which you speak to
    us.
But above all we thank you for your Son,
    Jesus Christ our Saviour,
    through whom we see you, our Father.
Let his Spirit dwell within us
    giving us the power to serve you with gladness
    all the days of our life;
through Jesus Christ our Lord. **Amen.**

*Minister.*

O God our Father, merciful and gracious, hear the
thanksgivings with which we come before thy
throne.
For the wonder of thy beauty manifest in the
world; and for thy fatherly care shown in provision
for our needs; praise be to thee;

*People.*
Praise be to thee, O God.

*Minister.*
For Jesus Christ thy Son, the Word incarnate, who came to end the reign of sin and death, and to bring in the reign of righteousness and life; praise be to thee;

*People.*
Praise be to thee, O God.

*Minister.*
For the energy of thy Holy Spirit, constantly at work in the church and in the world; and for the disclosure of thy glory to us through prophets, saints and benefactors; praise be to thee;

*People.*
Praise be to thee, O God.

*Minister.*
For the happiness of our earthly life; for home and friends; and for the joy of loving and being loved; praise be to thee;

*People.*
Praise be to thee, O God.

*Minister.*
For the power to love thee; for the right to pray to thee; and for thine answers to our prayers; praise be to thee;

*People.*
Praise be to thee, O God.

*Minister and People.*

Accept our praises, O Lord, for Christ's sake.

**Amen.**

*Minister.*

We thank you, O God, for you are gracious.

You have loved us from the beginning of time,
and you have remembered us when we were in
trouble.

*People.*

Your mercy endures forever.

*Minister.*

We thank you, O God, for you came to us in Jesus
Christ,
who has redeemed the world,
and saved us from our sins.

*People.*

Your mercy endures forever.

*Minister.*

We thank you, O God, for you sent us your Holy
Spirit,
to comfort us,
and to lead us into all truth.

*People.*

Your mercy endures for ever. **Amen.**


We thank you, God, for all the variety of the human race,
for the development and unfolding of human
character,
for the enrichment of our experiences by men

and women of every colour, language and belief,
and for our dependence on other people's skill, labour and love.
Most of all we thank you that Jesus lived a human life,
and became our example, our teacher and our Saviour.
Praise be to you, O God, now and always.   **Amen.**


*Minister.*
O God, we thank you for all great and simple joys:
For the gift of wonder, the joy of discovery and the everlasting freshness of experience;
*People.*
We thank you, God.

*Minister.*
For all that comes to us through sorrow and sympathy, through joy and achievement;
*People.*
We thank you, God.

*Minister.*
For musicians, poets and craftsmen; for all who work in form and colour to increase the beauty of life;
*People.*
We thank you, God.

*Minister.*
For the likeness of Christ in men and women, their forbearance, courage and kindness;

*People.*
We thank you, God.

*Minister.*
For faithful leaders and for all obscure and humble lives of service;

*People.*
We thank you, God.

*Minister and People.*
Glory be to you, Father, Son and Holy Spirit, now and forever.   **Amen.**

Gracious God, we thank you
    for the beauty of the mountains and the mystery
        of the plains,
    for the wealth of the waters, and the riches in
        mine and forest and field.
We thank you
    for those who turned back the wilderness and
        the solitude that their children might enjoy
        a secure home;
    for those who preached the gospel and strove
        to build the nation on the foundation of
        Jesus Christ.
We thank you
    for all who have toiled for liberty and peace,
        and have left us heirs of the opportunity they
        created.
Thanks be to you, O God, for the heritage you have given us. **Amen.**

Thanks be to thee, O God, for revealing thyself to men, and for sending forth thy messengers to every age: for the first apostles of Christ, sent into all the world to preach the gospel; for those who brought the good news to our land; for all who in ages of darkness kept alive the light, or in times of indifference were faithful to their Lord's command; for all thy followers in every age who have given their lives for the faith; for those in our day who have gone to the ends of the earth as heralds of thy love; for the innumerable company who now praise thee out of every kindred and nation and tongue. With these and with all thy people in earth and heaven we worship thee. **Amen.**

We thank thee, O Lord, for good and honest parents, gentle teachers, benefactors ever to be remembered, congenial companions, intelligent hearers, sincere friends, faithful servants: for all who have enriched us by their writings, sermons, conversations, prayers, examples, reproofs, injuries. For these and all other mercies we praise thee, we bless thee, we thank thee; through Jesus Christ our Lord. **Amen.**

### Church Anniversary

Almighty God, by whose inspiration our fathers built this church: we thank thee for bringing us to this hour of worship and this day of celebration. We honour thee for giving thy Son, who founded the church in his death and resurrection, and has sent it forth through the ages as a witness to thy love. We bless thee for bestowing thy Holy Spirit, who has hallowed this sanctuary and made it not only a place of beauty but a source of strength. We thank thee for calling men and women to serve thee, and for calling us in our time. Praise be to thee, O God, for thy work in our midst; through Jesus Christ our Lord. **Amen.**

## 10. INTERCESSIONS

### General Intercessions

O Lord, our God and Father, be graciously mindful of thy church, and deliver her from all evil. Strengthen and guard her through the word and sacraments, and perfect her in thy love. Bless her servants and their work. Be with those who suffer persecution for thy name's sake. Extend the boundaries of thy church, that the gospel of Christ may become known to all peoples. And gather her from the end of the earth to that kingdom which thou hast prepared.

Grant, O Lord, peace to the whole world, and let justice and righteousness rule on earth.

Grant in our homes and schools skill to bring up the young in thy fear. Preserve our country from harm and destruction. Grant that the earth may bear its fruit. Bless our labours, and grant that we may mutually serve one another. Protect our brothers on the sea and in other lands.

Come, O Lord, to all souls who seek thee. Hasten to the help of those who fight for their salvation. Care for those who are in danger and temptation, for the poor and sick, for the lonely and the oppressed; through Jesus Christ our Lord. **Amen.**

Father, you do not create us to live alone.
  You have not made us all alike.

We pray for our families,
  with whom we live day by day.
By all that we do and say
  help us to build up the faith and confidence of
    those we love.
When we quarrel, help us to forgive quickly.
Help us to welcome new members into our families without reserve, and not to neglect those
    who in our eyes have become less interesting
    or more demanding.

We pray for the places where we work,
  that there we may be workmen who have no
    need to be ashamed.
Whether those we work with be many or few,
  may we help to give them the sense that they
    are personally wanted and cared for.

We pray for the communities to which we belong,
  that we may be good citizens.
  Make us willing to accept responsibility when
    we are called to it;
  make us willing also to give place to others,
    that they too may have their opportunity.

We pray for the generation to which we belong,
  those with whom we share a common fund of
    memory, common standards of behaviour
    and a common attitude towards the world.

Grant that the presence of Christ may be so real
to us that we may be able to help our generation
to see him also as our contemporary.

Father, into whose world we come
and from whose world finally we must go:
we thank you for all those people,
great and humble,
who have maintained the fabric of the
world's life in the past and left us a great
inheritance.
May we take up and encourage what is good,
and hand it on to those who come after, believing that our work in your name will not be
wasted. **Amen.**

*Minister.*

Almighty God, our heavenly Father, who lovest all
and forgettest none, we bring to thee our prayers
for all thy children.
For all whom we love, and for whom we watch
and care;

*People.*

We beseech thee to hear us, O God.

*Minister.*

For all prisoners and captives, and all who suffer
from oppression, that thou wilt manifest thy mercy
towards them, and make the heart of man merciful as thine own;

*People.*

We beseech thee to hear us, O God.

*Minister.*

For all who bear the cross of suffering, the sick in body or in mind;

*People.*

We beseech thee to hear us, O God.

*Minister.*

For all those who are troubled by the sin or suffering of those they love;

*People.*

We beseech thee to hear us, O God.

*Minister.*

For all who are absorbed in their own grief, that they may be raised to share the sorrows of their brethren, and know the secret and blessed fellowship of the cross;

*People.*

We beseech thee to hear us, O God.

*Minister.*

For all perplexed by the deeper questions of life, and overshadowed with doubt, that light may arise in their darkness;

*People.*

We beseech thee to hear us, O God.

*Minister.*

For all who are tried by passionate temptations, or mean suggestions, that thy mercy may be their salvation;

*People.*
We beseech thee to hear us, O God.

*Minister.*
For all who are lonely and sad in the midst of others' joys, that they may know thee as their friend and comforter;
*People.*
We beseech thee to hear us, O God.

*Minister.*
For the infirm and aged, and for all who are passing through the valley of death, that they may find their strength in thee, and light at evening time;
*People.*
We beseech thee to hear us, O God.

*Minister.*
For all forgotten by us, but dear to thee;
*People.*
We beseech thee to hear us, O God.

*Minister and People.*
O God our Father, have regard to our intercessions, answer them according to thy will, and make us the channels of thine infinite pity and helpfulness and worthy to pray through Jesus Christ our Lord. **Amen.**

*Minister.*
Almighty God, who art the hearer and answerer of prayer and who hast bidden us be mindful of

all men and to pray for thy cause and kingdom, hear, we pray thee, our prayer of intercession.

For the holy catholic church throughout the world that in a day when clouds and darkness are round about us, she may show forth thy light and thy truth;

*People.*
We beseech thee to hear us.

*Minister.*
That the divisions which are her shame may be taken away and that drawing closer to thee, thy people may be drawn closer to one another in understanding and love;

*People.*
We beseech thee to hear us.

*Minister.*
That by the faithful preaching of thy word, thy sovereign will, thine over-ruling power and thy redeeming purpose may be made known to all men;

*People.*
We beseech thee to hear us.

*Minister.*
That to the farthest corner of the earth the glorious gospel of thy saving love may be proclaimed till at the name of Jesus every knee shall bow and every tongue confess that he is Lord;

*People.*
We beseech thee to hear us.

*Minister.*

That in the affairs of men and nations thy church may speak with the authority of her divine commission and that by the proclamation of thy solemn judgements, the constraint and summons of thy love, we may be led into the way of peace;

*People.*

We beseech thee to hear us.

*Minister.*

Bless we pray thee our sovereign lady, Queen Elizabeth and her royal house: prosper her reign and grant that being herself subject to him who is King of kings and Lord of the nations she may in all things show forth the strength and beauty of the faith and know thy peace.

*People.*

We beseech thee to hear us.

*Minister.*

Let thy blessing rest, O Lord, on all who bear the vast responsibilities of state; grant them wisdom to plan and strength to perform such things as shall be to the honour of thy name and the peace and order of the world.

*People.*

We beseech thee to hear us.

*Minister and People.*

Mercifully hear, O Lord God, this our prayer, for we offer it in the name and for the sake of Jesus Christ our Lord. **Amen.**

## 11. SPECIFIC INTERCESSIONS

### For the Church

O almighty God, who hast built thy church upon the foundation of the apostles and prophets, Jesus Christ himself being the head corner stone: grant us so to be joined together in unity of spirit by their doctrine, that we may be made an holy temple acceptable unto thee; through Jesus Christ our Lord. **Amen.**

Almighty God, whose purpose is that men should love thee and give themselves to thee, we pray for thy church. Stir it from its complacency, that it may bear witness to the world in simplicity and in truth. Fill it with thy Holy Spirit that, as in the days of Pentecost, men may be set afire with passion, and work for the final achievement of thy kingdom on earth. We pray in the name of him who is the head of the church, even Jesus Christ our Lord. **Amen.**

### For the Congregation

Ever-gracious God, who hast called men and women from near and far into the fellowship of thy church, watch over this congregation. Increase its members' zeal for thy kingdom; distribute among them the varied interests and abilities needed for effective witness; and unite them all in faith, hope and love; through Jesus Christ our Lord. **Amen.**

### For Ministers

Illumine, we pray thee, O God, all ministers of thy gospel with true knowledge and understanding of thy word, that, both by their preaching and their living, they may set it forth and show it accordingly; through Jesus Christ our Lord. **Amen.**

### For Those Training for Service in the Church

O Lord Jesus Christ, who dost command thy disciples to proclaim the glad tidings of thy saving love to all mankind: pour out thy Holy Spirit on all who are in training for service in thy church. Give them the seeing eye, the hearing ear, and the ready will to receive and preach thy glorious truth. Bless them with the spirit of discipline and concentration, and enable them to worship, to work, and to witness wherever they may be sent. Hear us, O loving Saviour, whom with the Father and the Holy Spirit we worship, ever one God, world without end. **Amen.**

### For the Unity of the Church

Eternal God, look mercifully upon the broken body of thy church. Draw its members unto thee and one to another by the band of thy love; that its restored unity may bring healing to the nations, and the life of mankind may glorify thee; through Jesus Christ our Lord. **Amen.**

O God, who biddest us to dwell with one mind in thine house: of thy mercy put away from us all that causes faction and bitterness, that, through thy bountiful goodness, we may keep the unity of the Spirit in the bond of peace; through Christ, the Prince of peace. **Amen.**

O Lord Jesus Christ, who didst say to thine apostles, "Peace I leave with you, my peace I give unto you"; regard not our sins but the faith of thy church, and grant it that peace and unity which is agreeable to thy will, who livest and reignest with the Father and the Holy Spirit, one God, world without end. **Amen.**

### For the World Council of Churches

O God, who art the Father of all peoples near and far, we pray for the World Council of Churches, that thou wilt use it to bring thy light to the nations and thy salvation to the ends of the earth. Sustain its leaders and office-bearers, direct those who maintain the work of its departments, and inspire those who speak in its name in the councils of men. Grant to them, and to all its members who have covenanted together, the continual help of thy Holy Spirit; that they may impart to us, and to thy whole church, new depths of understanding, new clarity of utterance, new visions of justice and peace, and new compassion for the suffering and oppressed. This we ask, for thy glory, O God, through Jesus Christ our Lord. **Amen.**

### For the Mission of the Church

Bestow, O Lord, thy heavenly grace upon all who are called to be fellow-workers with thee, that by them Christ may be lifted up in every land and all men be drawn to him. In times of loneliness and weariness cheer them with thy presence; in disappointment give them patience; in the press of affairs keep their spirits fresh; in difficulties and dangers uphold and protect them; in success keep them humble of heart; in failure strengthen them to persevere. Make them to be joyful in service, and at all times deepen in them the sense of dependence upon thee and give them peace in thy service; through Jesus Christ our Lord. **Amen.**

O thou who art the great Shepherd of the sheep, we pray for those who in thy service are ministering unto the needs of men. For doctors and nurses, for teachers and pastors, for those who go out into the highways and byways seeking those who need thy love, we ask thy continuing help and mercy. For those who serve in less noticed ways, for those who supply our daily needs, for those whom we do not see or know, but upon whom we rely to provide clothes to wear and food to eat, we ask thy continuing love and mercy. In their humble service may they show forth the love of him who came to love the world. **Amen.**

Almighty God, who hast called the church out of the world that she might bring the world to thee: make her faithful in the work thou hast entrusted to her hands. Bless and uphold thy servants who are gone forth in her name to preach the gospel in distant lands; be with them in all perils by land or by water, in weariness and painfulness, in discouragement and persecution; endue them with power from on high. Stir up the hearts of thy people here and everywhere, that by their prayers, gifts, and labours, they may have a part in the spreading of thy gospel over all the earth; and hasten the time when all the ends of the world shall remember and turn unto the Lord, and all the kindreds of the nations shall worship before thee; through Jesus Christ our Lord. **Amen.**

### For the Queen and Rulers

Almighty God, the fountain of all goodness, we humbly beseech thee to bless our sovereign lady, Queen Elizabeth, and all who are set in authority under her; that they may order all things in wisdom, righteousness, and peace, to the honour of thy holy name, and the good of thy church and people; through Jesus Christ our Lord. **Amen.**

### For Parliament

Most gracious God, we humbly beseech thee for the Houses of Parliament at this time assembled, that thou wouldest be pleased to direct and prosper all their counsels, to the advancement of thy glory, the good of thy church, and the safety, honour, and welfare of this land; to the end that peace and happiness, truth and justice, religion and piety, may be established among us for all generations; through Jesus Christ our Lord. **Amen.**

### For Rulers and Statesmen

O God, the Lord of all kings and kingdoms, let thy strong hand control the nations and cause them to long for thy love to rule on the earth. Strengthen the hands of all who are working for righteousness and peace. Guide the hearts and minds of all rulers and statesmen that they may seek first thy kingdom and the establishment of justice and freedom for all peoples, both small and great; through Jesus Christ our Lord. **Amen.**

### For the Peace of the World

Kindle, O God, the desire for peace in the hearts of all men, and guide the nations with thy wisdom; that thy kingdom may go forward in power, till the whole earth is filled with the knowledge of thy love; through Jesus Christ our Lord. **Amen.**

O God, who hast revealed to this generation wonders and mysteries of thy universe, forgive us that we have often turned our larger knowledge to foolish and cruel uses, and filled the world with terror and anguish. Increase in us all the power to dwell in peace together, settling our disputes without resort to violence, so that we may be able to put away the instruments of war, and use thy gifts, as thou dost will, to save life and not to destroy it; through Jesus Christ our Lord. **Amen.**

Eternal God, in whose perfect kingdom no sword is drawn but the sword of righteousness, and no strength known but the strength of love: so guide and inspire, we pray thee, the work of all who seek thy kingdom at home and abroad, that all peoples may seek and find their security, not in force of arms, but in the perfect love that casteth out fear, and in the fellowship revealed to us by thy Son, Jesus Christ our Lord. **Amen.**

O eternal God, in whose will is our peace: we commend unto thee the needs of all the world;

where there is hatred, give love; where there is injury, pardon; where there is doubt, faith; where there is despair, hope; where there is darkness, light; where there is sadness, joy; for thy mercy and thy truth's sake. **Amen.**

### For Foreign Policy

Teach us, O Lord, to see every question of foreign policy in the light of our faith, that we may check in ourselves and in others every temper which makes for war, all ungenerous judgments, all promptings of self-assurance, all presumptuous claims; that being ever ready to recognize the needs and aspirations of other nations, we may, with patience, do whatsoever in us lies to remove suspicions and misunderstandings; and to honour all men in Jesus Christ our Lord. **Amen.**

### For the United Nations

O God the Father of all, guide with thy Spirit those who lead in the nations of the world. Bless the United Nations Organization that through its means righteousness may be established in international relationships and a lasting peace ensured; through him who has shown to man the ways of righteousness, mercy and peace, thy Son, Jesus Christ, our Lord. **Amen.**

### For the Community

Almighty God, who hast ordained that men and women shall dwell together in communities, and that there they shall find their true relationship in mutual service, we pray thee to fill the hearts of all sections of this community with an unselfish sense of duty and of consideration for each other in the doing and demanding only of what is best for all, and that, being delivered from narrow visions and mere desire for gain, all may take pride in the opportunity and quality of their labour, and be ashamed to exploit in their own interests, the well-being of less fortunate people, but may seek only the rewards of righteousness and generosity; through Jesus Christ our Lord. **Amen.**

### For All Workers

*Minister.*

O God, who hast made us a royal priesthood, that we might offer unto thee prayer and intercession for all sorts and conditions of men, hear us as we pray.

For all who toil in the burden and the heat of day, that they may enjoy the rewards of their industry, that they may not be defrauded of their due, and that we may never cease to be mindful of our debt to them;

*People.*

We ask thy grace and pledge our concern, O God.

*Minister.*

For those who have authority and power over their fellow men, that they may not use it for selfish advantage, but be guided to do justice and to love mercy;

*People.*

We ask thy grace and pledge our concern, O God.

*Minister.*

For the rulers of the nations, that they may act wisely and without pride, may seek to promote peace among the peoples and establish justice in our common life;

*People.*

We ask thy grace and pledge our concern, O God.

*Minister.*

For teachers and ministers of the word, for artists and interpreters of our spiritual life, that they may rightly divide the word of truth, and not be tempted by pride or greed or any ignoble passion to corrupt the truth to which they are committed;

*People.*

We ask thy grace and pledge our concern, O God.

*Minister.*

For prophets and seers and saints, who awaken us from our sloth, that they may continue to hold their torches high in a world darkened by prejudice and sin, and ever be obedient to the heavenly vision;

*People.*

We ask thy grace and pledge our concern, O God.

*Minister and People.*

O Lord, who hast bound us together in this bundle of life, give us grace to understand how our lives depend upon the courage, the industry, the honesty and integrity of our fellow men; that we may be mindful of their needs, grateful for their faithfulness, and faithful in our responsibilities to them; through Jesus Christ our Lord. **Amen.**

Eternal Creator, we bring before thee in our prayers all those who labour with their hands; those who create works of beauty; those who labour in the menial tasks of daily life; those who face the dull monotony of constant repetition. For men whose vision seldom rises above the commonplace, we ask that thou wilt stand by them in their toil, bringing to them the awareness that even the dull, the dismal, and the difficult cannot separate them from thy love; in the name of him who was the carpenter of Nazareth. **Amen.**

### For Teachers and Learners

O Lord Jesus Christ, who wast found in the temple listening to the teachers and asking them questions: be with us who are assembled in thy name; and grant to those who teach, and to those who learn, a right understanding of thy holy word, and a readiness to hear and do thy blessed will; who livest and reignest with the Father and the Holy Spirit, one God, world without end. **Amen.**

### For Teachers

Lord Jesus Christ, who didst show on this earth thy love for children: guide, we pray thee, with thy Spirit, those who are called to teach in this land; that nothing may hinder our children from growing in faith and love towards thee, and that thy name may be honoured both in our schools and in our homes. **Amen.**

Grant, we pray thee, O Lord, to all who teach in our schools thy Spirit of wisdom and grace to enable them to lead their students to reverence truth, to desire goodness, and to rejoice in beauty; so that, following after these things, both those who learn and those who teach may come to know and worship thee, the Giver of all that is good; through Jesus Christ our Lord. **Amen.**

### For Universities and Colleges

Bless, O Lord, the universities and colleges of this and other lands, that both teachers and students may be governed by a true love of learning and may, by thy grace, possess that integrity which alone can bring them to knowledge of the truth. Let them never, for lack of courage, refuse to face the facts. Let them never, for personal advantage, conceal the truth, nor, in pursuit of power, betray it; and lead them to those depths of thought and obedience where alone thou canst make thyself known unto them. **Amen.**

### For Scientists

O holy God, source of all wisdom and truth, enlighten all men of science who search out the secrets of thy creation, that their humility before nature may be matched by reverence towards thee. Save us from misusing their labours, that the forces they set free may enrich the life of man, and that thy name may be hallowed both in the search for truth and in the use of power. **Amen.**

**For Speakers and Writers**

Almighty God, who hast proclaimed thine eternal truth by the voice of prophets and evangelists: direct and bless, we pray thee, those who in our generation speak where many listen and write what many read; that they may do their part in making the heart of this people wise, its mind sound, and its will righteous; through Christ our Lord. **Amen.**

**For Industry, Commerce, Labour**

O Lord Jesus Christ, who in thy earthly life didst share man's toil, and hallow the labour of his hands: prosper all who maintain the industries of this land and give them pride in their work, a just reward, and joy both in supplying need and in serving thee; who with the Father and the Holy Spirit livest and reignest, ever one God, world without end. **Amen.**

**For Manual Workers**

O God our heavenly Father, hear us on behalf of all who live by strength of arm or skill of hand: those who till the earth; those who toil in mines; those whose business is in the deep waters; those who labour at furnaces and in factories; those who work in dangerous trades. We pray, O Father, that thou wilt comfort, sustain, protect and support them; through Jesus Christ our Lord. **Amen.**

**For Farmers**

Almighty God, who hast blessed the earth that it should be fruitful and bring forth abundantly whatsoever is needful for the life of man: prosper the labours of the farmer, and grant such seasonable weather that we may gather in the fruits of the earth, and ever rejoice in thy goodness, to the praise of thy holy name; through Jesus Christ our Lord. **Amen.**

### For Fishermen

Almighty God, who hast made the sea and all that moveth therein: bestow thy blessing on the harvest of the waters, that it may be abundant in its season, and on our fishermen, that they may be safe in every peril of the deep; so that we all with thankful hearts may acknowledge thee, who art the Lord of the sea and of the dry land; through Jesus Christ our Lord. **Amen.**

### For Sailors and Those Who Serve Their Needs

Unto Thee, O God, do we commit all sailors and those who serve their needs; the officers and men of the Navy; all lighthouse-keepers, coastguards, and pilots; the men of the fishing fleets and the crews of lifeboats; the workers in docks and harbours; and all who care for sailors and their families; that all who know the peril of the sea may also know the succour of thy love. **Amen.**

### For Homemakers

O God, who givest to each one his work, and through our labours dost accomplish thy purposes upon earth; grant thy blessing, we pray thee, to all who work at home. Let them remember that in ministering to the needs of others they are serving thee; that seeking first thy kingdom and righteousness, all things may be added unto them here and hereafter; through Jesus Christ our Lord. **Amen.**

### For Children

Heavenly Father, whose care is for all thy children: we pray for those who are young. As they grow in stature, may they grow in knowledge of thy love. Provide them with loving homes and concerned friends, that they may ever participate in the riches of thy love. Where children are hungry, and naked, and sick, and in prison, send out thy servants of compassion to bring health and strength, warmth and direction; through him who was once a boy in Nazareth. **Amen.**

### For the Aged

With grateful hearts we remember those in our midst who, now in their twilight years, give unto us wisdom and strength for our way. We pray, O God, that thou wilt never forget them, but wilt keep them in thy care and bless them with thy presence, that they may look forward in peace and find in that which is to come the knowledge of thy love. **Amen.**

### For Travellers

Almighty God, who art the sure guide and strong refuge of all who put their trust in thee: we ask thee to watch over all travellers by land or sea or air, and to give them thy favour and protection. Go with them where they go; dwell with them where they dwell; preserve them from all evils and dangers on their way; and of thy mercy bring them again to their homes and friends in peace; through Jesus Christ our Lord. **Amen.**

### For Absent Friends

O heavenly Father, who has bestowed upon us the comfort of earthly friends: look in love upon those dear to us from whom we are separated. Protect them and keep them from all harm; prosper and bless them in all good things; suffer them never to be desolate or afraid; but in thine own good time may we renew the fellowship of sight and hand; through Jesus Christ our Lord. **Amen.**

### For Immigrants and Visitors from Abroad

O God, the Father of all men, who hast bidden thy people to show kindness to the stranger: we pray for those who come from other countries to make their homes or to study in this land; help them and us to overcome the difficulties of custom, language and race; surround them with companions who welcome and befriend them; and bless the societies that foster understanding and goodwill; that in thy great family we may live as members one of another; through Jesus Christ our Lord. **Amen.**

### For Those in Trouble

We remember before Thee, O God, those who bear crosses alone: the sick and infirm suffering on beds of pain, parents troubled by their wayward children, homes where alcohol and lust have created tension and heartbreak, all those who are plagued with secret sins and who know not how to escape. Sustain these, thy children, with thine everlasting arms; through the mists and storms of this world may they catch a glimpse of the final fulfilment of thy purpose and the triumph of thy grace; through Christ our Lord. **Amen.**

Comfort, we beseech thee, most gracious God, all who are cast down and fearful of heart amid the sickness and sorrow of the world; and grant that, being strengthened by thy Holy Spirit, they may go on their way with confidence and hope; through Jesus Christ our Lord. **Amen.**

Be mindful, O God, of all who stand in need of thy great tenderness of heart, whether friend or foe or stranger; for thou art the help of the helpless, the hope of the hopeless, the Saviour of the tempest-tossed, and the God and Father of our Lord Jesus Christ. **Amen.**

### For the Sick

Have mercy, O Lord, upon all who are afflicted in body, mind or spirit; relieve their distress, comfort and cheer them in weariness or depression. Let thy presence be near them by day and night; for the sake of Jesus Christ our Lord. **Amen.**

Almighty Father, giver of life and health: look mercifully on the sick and suffering, that by thy blessing upon them, and upon those who minister to them, they may be restored, if it be thy gracious will, to health of body and mind, and give thanks to thee; through Jesus Christ our Lord. **Amen.**

**For the Suffering**

Lord God, you love us.
So we bring our prayers to you:
 for those who suffer pain;
 for those whose minds are disturbed, or have
  never matured;
 for those who have not had the opportunity to
  realize their potentialities;
 for those who are satisfied with something less
  than the life for which they were made;
 for those who know their guilt, their shallow-
  ness, their need, but who do not know of
  Jesus;
 for those who know that they must shortly die;
 for those who cannot wait to die.
Lord God, your Son has taken all our sufferings
 upon himself and has transformed them.
Help us, who offer these prayers, to take the
 sufferings of others upon ourselves, and so, by
 your grace, become the agents of your
 transforming love.
Through Jesus Christ our Lord. **Amen.**

**For the Handicapped**

Almighty Father, whose blessed Son, Jesus Christ,
went about doing good, opening the eyes of the
blind, loosing the tongue of the dumb, and un-
stopping the ears of the deaf: we bring to thee all
those who are likewise afflicted. Let thy voice be
heard in the hearts of those who cannot hear: let
the beauty of thy presence be visible to the souls
of those who cannot see: let thy word be spoken

through the lives of those who cannot speak; through Jesus Christ our Lord. **Amen.**

### For Those in Distress of Body, Mind and Heart

O thou who art love, and who seest all the suffering, injustice, and misery of this world: look mercifully upon the poor, the oppressed, and all who are heavy laden with error, labour, or sorrow. Fill our hearts with deep compassion for those who suffer, and hasten the coming of thy kingdom of justice and truth; for the sake of Jesus Christ our Lord. **Amen.**

### For Those Not Equal to Their Tasks

Grant thy help, O Lord, to all who feel ill-equipped for the demands life makes on them, whether through age or illness, tiredness or poverty. Sustain them in over-work and anxiety. Give them friends in their need, and enable them to find thy will in changed circumstances, and to rejoice in thy love even amid hardship and difficulty; through Jesus Christ our Lord. **Amen.**

### For the Unemployed

O Lord, our heavenly Father; we commend to thy protecting care and compassion the men and women of our land now suffering distress and anxiety through lack of work. Support and strengthen them. Guide those who direct the affairs of industry that thy people may be set free from want and fear, and be enabled to work in security and peace, for the relief of their necessities, and for the well-being of the realm; through Jesus Christ our Lord. **Amen.**

### For the Hungry

Eternal God, who hast promised seedtime and harvest as long as the world shall endure, we entreat thee on behalf of those in many lands who hunger while we have abundance. Support them in their trials, open our hearts to their needs, and grant that we may so use thy gifts of knowledge and understanding that the earth may yield a greater increase and that all may share in thy bounty; through Jesus Christ our Lord. **Amen.**

### For Suffering Children

O God, the Father of all, we commend to thy ceaseless compassion all homeless children and orphans, and all thy little ones whose lives are overshadowed by violence, or thwarted by disease and cruelty. Awaken in us thy living charity, that we may not rest while children cry for bread or go uncomforted for lack of love; through Jesus Christ our Lord. **Amen.**

### For Prisoners

O most merciful Father, who didst send thy Son Jesus Christ to proclaim deliverance to the captives, and to set at liberty them that are bruised: remember, we pray, all who are in captivity, prisons, and bitter bondage. In loneliness cheer them, in sickness relieve them; and fill them continually with the hope of thy everlasting mercy; through Jesus Christ our Lord. **Amen.**

### For Those Who Mourn

Comfort, O Lord, all who mourn for the loss of

those near and dear to them; be with them in their sorrow; give them faith to look beyond the troubles of the present time, and to know that neither life nor death can separate us from thy love which is in Jesus Christ our Lord. **Amen.**

### For Victims of a Disaster

Almighty Father, who hast set our lives on a planet where both beauty and danger are to be found, hear our prayer for those who have been overtaken by the disastrous (famine, flood, earthquake, fire, plague) in . . . . . . . . . . . . . . . . . .

Comfort the maimed and suffering; fortify with a sense of thy presence all who are overcome by fear and distress. Watch with those who anxiously watch. Draw thou near to the dying and bless them with thy peace. Sustain and uphold the bereaved. Endue with tenderness and strength the doctors and nurses, and all who help them minister to human need. And grant that we, our hearts moved by compassion like thine own, may share the burdens of these our brothers and so fulfil the law of Christ, thy Son our Lord. **Amen.**

### For Areas of Strife

Eternal Father, in whose hand are all the corners of the earth, we remember before thee those who live in areas of war or civil strife, especially in . . . . . . . . . . . . Be thou a shelter to the homeless, a protector to the helpless, a deliverer to the captive, and a comforter to the bereaved; through Jesus Christ our Lord. **Amen.**

**For Those Who Suffer in War**

Almighty God, Father of all men, we bring before thee in prayer those of every nation who are suffering through war; those who have been wounded or disabled, and those who have been bereaved; those who face mental suffering because of things they have seen or endured; all families separated by distance, and homes broken by sin; all the starving and homeless multitudes of our world. Give us a heart of compassion, O Lord, that by prayer and action we may help those who are working to relieve their needs; through Jesus Christ our Lord. **Amen.**

O God, who hast promised that they who wait upon thee shall renew their strength, we commend unto thee all who suffer through war and strife; the wounded, the sick, and the prisoners; the homeless, the hungry, and the oppressed; the anxious, the frightened, and the bereaved. Strengthen them, O Lord, with thy Holy Spirit, and give them friends to help them; we ask it is in his name, who bore for us the agony of the cross, thy Son, our Lord Jesus Christ. **Amen.**

**For Those Who Neglect God**

We pray for any who neglect you, Father:
for any who have gone the wrong way,
especially those who have brought trouble on themselves and others.
Take from them all blindness and stubbornness.
Give them hope and strength to begin again.

And make other people loving and wise enough
to help them. **Amen.**

### For the Ministry of Healing

O Lord Jesus Christ, who in thy life on earth didst
heal both the souls and the bodies of men: guide
all who now minister to body or to soul, and grant
that those who serve things spiritual may not despise the body, nor those who treat the body set at
nought the soul; but that, patiently seeking to
understand the unity of our human nature, they
may work together for the cure of all sickness and
disease, and for the recovery of that true health
which is thy gift to those who wait upon thee.

**Amen.**

Almighty God, whose blessed Son Jesus Christ
went about doing good, and healing all kinds of
sickness and disease among the people: continue
this his gracious work among us, especially in the
hospitals of our land; cheer, heal, and comfort
the sick; grant to the physicians, surgeons, and
nurses wisdom and skill, sympathy and patience;
and send down thy blessing on all who labour to
prevent suffering and to forward thy purposes of
love; through Jesus Christ our Lord. **Amen.**

### For Social Workers

O God, our heavenly Father, who knowest our
needs and dost care for us all, we pray for those
who give counsel and help to their fellow men: for
probation officers and all other social workers;
for all who by their skill and training ease the

burden of the aged, the lonely and the perplexed, and guide those who have missed the right way. Grant that these workers may have both wisdom and sympathy, and see men through the eyes of Christ, who beheld the multitudes distressed and scattered, as sheep not having a shepherd; through the same Jesus Christ our Lord. **Amen.**

**For Others**

Hear our prayer, Father,
for all in whom trust has been placed,
all to whom power is given,
all from whom love is asked,
all through whom wisdom is sought,
and all by whom joy can come
because of Jesus our Lord. **Amen.**

## 12. SUPPLICATIONS

Merciful God, to thee we commend ourselves and all those who need thy help and correction.
Where there is hatred, give love;
where there is injury, pardon;
where there is doubt, faith;
where there is despair, hope;
where there is sadness, joy;
where there is darkness, light.
Grant that we may not seek so much to be consoled, as to console;
to be understood, as to understand;
to be loved, as to love;
For in giving we receive, in pardoning we are pardoned, and dying we are born into eternal life. **Amen.**

May the strength of God pilot us.

May the power of God preserve us.

May the wisdom of God instruct us.

May the hand of God protect us.

May the way of God direct us.

May the shield of God defend us.

May the host of God guard us against the snares of evil and the temptations of the world.

May Christ be with us, Christ before us, Christ in us, Christ over us.

May thy salvation, O Lord, be always ours this day and for evermore. **Amen.**

God, our life-giver and liberator, make us both alert and free in your service.

In the light of your truth may we see what value to set on each day's events, and how best to deploy our resources for each day's decisions.

Help us to be hard-headed without becoming hard-hearted: and if we have to choose between two evils, give us at least the will to do right, and the assurance that even when we are at our wits' end we are never out of your mercy's reach.

Through Jesus Christ our Lord. **Amen.**

O God, the strength of all them that put their trust in thee: mercifully accept our prayers; and because through the weakness of our mortal nature we can do no good thing without thee, grant us the help of thy grace, that in keeping of thy commandments we may please thee both in will and deed; through Jesus Christ our Lord. **Amen.**

May thy hand direct us; thy strength empower us; thy wisdom enlighten us; thy grace be sufficient for us; thy love remove all fear from us; through Jesus Christ our Lord. **Amen.**

Father,
as we go to our homes and our work this coming
    week
we ask you to send the Holy Spirit into our lives.

    Open our ears   —to hear what you are saying to us in the things that happen to us and in the people we meet.

    Open our eyes   —to see the needs of the people round us.

    Open our hands—to do our work well, to help when help is needed.

    Open our lips   —to tell others the good news of Jesus and bring comfort, happiness and laughter to other people.

    Open our minds—to discover new truth about you and the world.

    Open our hearts—to love you and our fellow men as you have loved us in Jesus.

To him, with you our Father and the Holy Spirit, one God,
all honour and praise shall be given
now and for ever. **Amen.**

Grant unto us, O God, the fulness of thy promises: where we have been weak, grant us thy strength; where we have been confused, grant us thy guidance; where we have been distraught, grant us thy comfort; where we have been dead, grant us thy life. Apart from thee, O Lord, we are nothing. In and with thee we can do all things. **Amen.**

Lord Jesus Christ,
    you are the light of the world:
    light up our lives when we are in darkness.

In the darkness of our uncertainty—
    when we don't know what to do,
    when decisions are hard to take:
Lord, give us light to guide us.

In the darkness of our anxiety—
    when we are worried about what the future may
      bring,
    when we don't know where to turn:
Lord, give us the light of your peace.

In the darkness of our despair—
    when life seems empty,
    when we feel there is no point in going on:
Lord, give us the light of your hope.
In your name we ask it. **Amen.**

O God, we dedicate ourselves to thy tasks among men. Use us as thou wilt. Make us peacemakers in occasions of strife. Help us to love in times of tension. Give us power and confidence in times of doubt. Strengthen us to lead men in the way of thy word. Enable us to accept the baptism with which Christ was baptized; in whose name we pray. **Amen.**

### For Love Toward God

O God, who hast prepared for them that love thee such good things as pass man's understanding: pour into our hearts such love towards thee, that we, loving thee above all things, may obtain thy promises, which exceed all we can desire; through Jesus Christ our Lord. **Amen.**

### For the Spirit of Neighbourliness

Increase, O God, the spirit of neighbourliness among us: that in peril we may uphold one another, in calamity serve one another, in suffering tend one another, and in homelessness, loneliness, or exile befriend one another; through Jesus Christ our Lord. **Amen.**

### For Loving Hearts

Set our hearts on fire with love for you, O God, that in its flame we may love you with all our heart, with all our mind, with all our soul and with all our strength, and our neighbours as ourselves, so that keeping your commandments, we may glorify you, the giver of all good gifts; through Jesus Christ our Lord. **Amen.**

### For a Blessing on Our Work

O God our Father, who hast set us in thy good world to replenish and subdue it, grant that in our daily work we may glorify thee, satisfy ourselves, and serve others. Deliver us from laziness and irresponsibility, from pride and self-importance. Enable us to work hard and to relax creatively, to strive unceasingly for the welfare of all and to rest peacefully when our work is done; through Jesus Christ our Lord. **Amen.**

### For Adequacy

O God, come to us with the resources of your power, that we may be strong within. We ask not for easy lives, but for adequacy. We ask not to be freed from storms, but to build our houses on rock that will not fall. We pray not for a smooth sea, but for a stout ship, a good compass, and a strong heart; through Jesus Christ our Lord. **Amen.**

### For Delight in Simple Things

O God, you made the heavens and the earth and all that is good and lovely, and in your Son have shown us that the secret of joy is a heart free from selfish desires: help us to delight in simple things, and to rejoice in the beauties which abound in your creation; through Jesus Christ our Lord.

**Amen.**

### For Loyalty to Truth

Our Father, in times of doubts and questionings, when our belief is perplexed by new learning, new teaching, new thought, when our faith is strained by creeds, by doctrines, by mysteries beyond our understanding: give us the faithfulness of learners and the courage of believers in you; give us boldness to examine, and faith to trust all truth; patience and insight to master difficulties; stability to hold fast our traditions with enlightened interpretations, to admit all fresh truth made known to us, and in times of trouble to grasp new knowledge and to combine it loyally and honestly with the old. Save us and help us, we humbly ask, O Lord. **Amen.**

### For Wisdom

Grant us, O Lord, to know what is worth knowing, to love what is worth loving, to praise what can bear with praise, to hate what in your sight is unworthy, to prize what to you is precious, and, above all, to search out and to do what is well-pleasing to you; through Jesus Christ our Lord. **Amen.**

### For Help in Daily Living

O God, who givest all good things and who knowest what we need before we ask, we come to thee with confidence as children to a father able and willing to help us. Grant us, O Lord, in all our duties thy help; in all our difficulties thy counsel; in all our trials, thy protection; and in all our ways, thy guidance and blessing; through Jesus Christ our Lord. **Amen.**

### Before any Undertaking

Go before us, O Lord, in all our doings, with thy most gracious favour, and further us with thy continual help; that in all our works, begun, continued, and ended in thee, we may glorify thy holy name, and finally by thy mercy obtain everlasting life; through Jesus Christ our Lord. **Amen.**

### In the Morning

O Lord, our heavenly Father, almighty and everlasting God, who hast safely brought us to the beginning of this day: defend us in the same with thy mighty power; and grant that this day we fall into no sin, neither run into any kind of danger; but that all our doings may be ordered by thy governance, to do always that is righteous in thy sight; through Jesus Christ our Lord. **Amen.**

### In the Evening

Watch thou, dear Lord, with those who wake, or watch, or weep tonight, and give thine angels charge over those who sleep. Tend thy sick ones, O Lord Christ. Rest thy weary ones. Bless the dying ones. Soothe the suffering ones. Pity thine afflicted ones. Shield thy joyous ones. And all, for thy love's sake. **Amen.**

Lighten our darkness, we beseech thee, O Lord; and by thy great mercy defend us from all perils and dangers of this night; for the love of thy only Son, our Saviour, Jesus Christ. **Amen.**

## 13. COMMEMORATION OF THE DEPARTED

Eternal God, before whose face the generations rise and pass away: we rejoice in the communion of thy saints. We remember all who have faithfully lived and died, especially those most dear to us. Lift us into life and love; give us at last a place among those who have trusted in thee, and have striven in all things to do thy will. And to thy name, with the church on earth and the church in heaven, we ascribe all honour and glory, world without end. **Amen.**

Eternal God, Creator and Lover of all men, we praise thee for all those who have kept the faith and made their witness for Christ, upholding truth, resisting evil and labouring for liberty, justice and brotherhood. Grant that their devotion may bring forth good fruit in this generation and in the generations to come; through Jesus Christ our Lord. **Amen.**

Almighty and everlasting Father, with whom do live those who have loved and served thee: we thank thee for them. We bless thee that through faith and patience they have inherited thy promises and are now with thee in joy and peace. Grant that we may follow Christ encouraged by their example; and that we, with all who have lived in thy faith and favour, may be gathered into thy kingdom for ever; through the grace and mercy of Jesus Christ our Saviour. **Amen.**

Our heavenly Father, we rejoice in the communion of thy saints. We remember before thee all who have departed this life in thy faith and love, and especially those most dear to us. We thank thee for our fellowship with them, and for the promise of future joy. Grant that following their example of Christian living, we may run the race that is set before us, and with them ever worship and adore thy glorious name; through Jesus Christ our Lord. **Amen.**

Eternal God, the faithful Creator and Lover of all men, we praise thee for all who have laboured for liberty, justice and brotherhood; for those who have given themselves in defence of freedom, mercy and good faith among the nations; for those who in life and death have quickened our lives, and through whose sacrifice we live. Grant that, holding the dead in continual remembrance, we may walk with cleansed hearts, strengthened wills, and faith confirmed in the way that leads to life; through Jesus Christ our Lord. **Amen.**

Almighty God, we remember before you those who have lived among us, who have directed our steps in the way, opened our eyes to the truth, inspired our hearts by their witness, and strengthened our wills by their devotion. We rejoice in their lives dedicated to your service, we honour them in their death, and we pray that we may be united with them in the glory of Christ's resurrection. **Amen.**

## 14. COMMISSIONS

Go into the world in the power of the Holy Spirit to fulfil your high calling as servants and soldiers of Jesus Christ.

Go forth and make disciples of all nations, baptizing them in the name of the Father and of the Son and of the Holy Spirit, teaching them to observe all that Christ has commanded you; and lo, he is with you always, to the close of the age.

*Matthew 28.19, 20 (adapted)*

Let your light so shine before men, that they may
see your good works and give glory to your Father
who is in heaven.                    *Matthew 5.16*

You are ambassadors for Christ,
God making his appeal through you.
                          *II Corinthians 5.20 (adapted)*

Be alert; stand firm in the faith; be valiant and
strong. Let all you do be done in love.
                          *I Corinthians 16. 13, 14*

Go out into the world in peace. Be brave; keep
hold of what is good; never pay back wrong for
wrong; encourage the fainthearted; support the
weak and the distressed; give due honour to everyone. Be always joyful; pray continually; give thanks
whatever happens; for this is what God in Christ
wills for you.           *I Thessalonians 5.14-18 (adapted)*

Christ within you,
    the hope of glory to come.
Go into the world
    with a daring and tender love.
The world is waiting.
Go in peace.
And all that you do
    do it for love,
    and by the Spirit of Jesus
    who is the Lord.

Be strong and of good courage, do not be afraid:
for it is the Lord your God who goes with you, he
will not fail you or forsake you.
                          *Deuteronomy 31.6 (adapted)*

## 15. BENEDICTIONS

The grace of the Lord Jesus Christ and the love of God and the fellowship of the Holy Spirit be with you all. **Amen.**

*II Corinthians 13.14*

The Lord bless you, and keep you.
the Lord make his face to shine upon you, and be gracious unto you:
the Lord lift up his countenance upon you, and give you peace. **Amen.**

*Numbers 6. 24-27*

The peace of God, which passeth all understanding, keep your hearts and minds in the knowledge and love of God, and of his Son Jesus Christ our Lord; and the blessing of God almighty, the Father, the Son, and the Holy Spirit, be amongst you and remain with you always. **Amen.**

Now the God of peace, that brought again from the dead our Lord Jesus, that great Shepherd of the sheep, through the blood of the everlasting covenant, make you perfect in every good work to do his will, working in you that which is well-pleasing in his sight, through Jesus Christ; to whom be glory for ever and ever. **Amen.**

Grace, mercy and peace from God the Father, Son, and Holy Spirit, be with you for ever. **Amen.**

Peace be to you, and love with faith, from God the Father and the Lord Jesus Christ. **Amen.**

*Ephesians 6.23 (adapted)*

The peace of God rule in your hearts, and the words of Christ dwell in you richly in all wisdom. **Amen.**

Go in peace; and the blessing of God almighty, the Father, the Son, and the Holy Spirit, rest upon you, and remain with you always. **Amen.**

God grant you progress and joy in the faith. **Amen.**
*Philippians 1.25 (adapted)*

The grace of Christ attend you,
the love of God surround you,
the Holy Spirit keep you. **Amen.**

God the Father bless you and keep you,
God the Son save you and direct you,
God the Spirit teach you and guide you,
    this day and evermore. **Amen.**

# III. OCCASIONAL SERVICES

## 1. MARRIAGE

### Introduction

The solemnization of marriage is a civil contract. The minister has the authority of the civil law and is responsible for seeing that the conditions required by the state are fulfilled. For Christian people, marriage is also a religious rite. The minister has authority from the church and is responsible for seeing that the service reflects the faith of the church. This order for the solemnization of marriage complies with the Marriage Acts of the provinces of Canada and is arranged as a service for public worship.

The structure of the service is that of Approach, Word of God and Response. In the Approach there is a hymn, scripture sentence and a prayer of approach. In each of these man's dependence upon God is acknowledged. Statements required by law concerning marriage are also made in this section. The Word of God is proclaimed in the reading of passages selected from the Old and the New Testaments and in the exhortation. This exhortation is a statement of the doctrine of marriage and may take the place of a sermon or commentary. The third part of the service is the Response by the persons to be married and by the congregation. The man and the woman make their marriage vows and symbolize this by the giving and receiving of a ring. The whole congregation responds in prayers of thanksgiving, intercession and supplication. The service concludes with a hymn and a blessing.

Although the rubrics in the service are explicit, the structure and furnishings of the church will usually determine what procedures are followed. A rehearsal helps to assure that the service will move forward with dignity.

The principles governing the choice of music are those that govern the choice for any service of worship. Whatever is suitable for one is suitable for the other. All that is sung or played should be an offering in praise of God.

AN OUTLINE FOR

## THE SOLEMNIZATION OF MARRIAGE

*The Approach*  Processional Hymn
Scripture Sentences
Admonition
Prayer of Approach

*The Word*  Epistle
*of God*  Psalm
Gospel
Address

*The Response*  Invocation of the Holy Spirit
Questions and Vows
Declaration
Prayers of Thanksgiving and Intercession
Lord's Prayer
Hymn
Blessing

AN ORDER FOR

## THE SOLEMNIZATION OF MARRIAGE

*The laws respecting the solemnization of marriage, whether by publishing the banns in churches or by licence, being different in the several provinces, each minister is required to know and observe the laws of his own province.*

*When banns are published they shall be read in the church on one or more Sundays before the day appointed for the marriage, as the laws of the province may require.*

*Where no specific form of banns is ordered by law, the minister shall say,*

I publish the banns of marriage between

N.          *Christian names and surname*

of . . . . . . . . . . . . . . Church, in the . . . . . . . . . . . . .

of . . . . . . . . . . . . . . . . . . . . . . . . . . . . . . . . . . . . . , and

N.          *Christian names and surname*

of . . . . . . . . . . . . . . Church, in the . . . . . . . . . . . . .

of . . . . . . . . . . . . . . . . . . . . . . . . . . . . . . . . . . . . . . ,

If any of you know just cause why these two persons should not be joined in marriage, you are to declare it to me. Pray that they may enter into this union in the name of the Lord, and be blessed.

*When the people are assembled the service may begin with the processional hymn* Praise, my soul, the King of heaven, *or another suitable hymn such as* Praise to the Lord, the Almighty, the King of creation *or* Now thank we all our God, *during which the bridal party shall enter the church. The persons to be married shall stand side by side, the man on the right of the woman. At the conclusion of the hymn the minister shall say,*

Unless the Lord builds the house, those who build it labour in vain.

*Psalm 127.1*

In all your ways acknowledge him, and he will make straight your paths.

*Proverbs 3.6*

*The minister shall say to the persons being married,*

N. *Christian names and surname* and N. *Christian names and surname*

you have made known your desire to be married, and no one has shown just cause why you may not. If either of you know any lawful impediment why you may not be married, I charge you before God, the Searcher of all hearts, to declare it.

*If no impediment be stated, a prayer of approach shall follow,*
Almighty and everlasting God, in whom we live and move and have our being: grant unto us purity of heart and strength of purpose, so that no selfish desire may hinder us from knowing thy will, and no weakness from doing it; that in thy light we may see light, and in thy service find perfect freedom; through Jesus Christ our Lord. **Amen.**

*The people shall be seated and one or more of the following lessons shall be read,*
I Corinthians 13.4-8a
Love is patient and kind; love is not jealous or boastful; it is not arrogant or rude. Love does not insist on its own way; it is not irritable or resentful; it does not rejoice at wrong, but rejoices in the right. Love bears all things, believes all things, hopes all things, endures all things. Love never ends.

Ephesians 3.14-19

For this reason I bow my knees before the Father, from whom every family in heaven and on earth is named, that according to the riches of his glory he may grant you to be strengthened with might through his Spirit in the inner man, and that Christ may dwell in your hearts through faith; that you, being rooted and grounded in love, may have power to comprehend with all the saints what is the breadth and length and height and depth, and to know the love of Christ which surpasses knowledge, that you may be filled with all the fulness of God.

I John 4.7-13

Dear friends, let us love one another, because love is from God. Everyone who loves is a child of God and knows God, but the unloving know nothing of God. For God is love; and his love was disclosed to us in this, that he sent his only Son into the world to bring us life. The love I speak of is not our love for God, but the love he showed to us in sending his Son as the remedy for the defilement of our sins. If God thus loved us, dear friends, we in turn are bound to love one another. Though God has never been seen by any man, God himself dwells in us if we love one another; his love is brought to perfection within us. Here is the proof that we dwell in him and he dwells in us: he has imparted his Spirit to us.

*The people may sing or say,*

Psalm 100

Make a joyful noise to the Lord, all the lands!
Serve the Lord with gladness!
Come into his presence with singing!

Know that the Lord is God!
It is he that made us, and we are his;
    we are his people, and the sheep of his pasture.

Enter his gates with thanksgiving, and his courts
    with praise!
Give thanks to him, bless his name!

For the Lord is good;
    his steadfast love endures forever,
    and his faithfulness to all generations.

Psalm 121

I lift up my eyes to the hills.
From whence does my help come?
My help comes from the Lord,
    who made heaven and earth.

He will not let your foot be moved,
    he who keeps you will not slumber.
Behold, he who keeps Israel
    will neither slumber nor sleep.

The Lord is your keeper;
    the Lord is your shade
    on your right hand.
The sun shall not smite you by day,
    nor the moon by night.

**The Lord will keep you from all evil;**
**he will keep your life.**
**The Lord will keep your going out and your**
**coming in**
**from this time forth and for evermore.**

*At the conclusion of the psalm shall be sung or said,*

**Glory be to the Father,**
**and to the Son,**
**and to the Holy Spirit;**
**as it was in the beginning,**
**is now, and ever shall be:**
**world without end. Amen.**

*This lesson from the gospel may be read,*

John 15.9-12

Jesus said: "As the Father has loved me, so have I loved you; abide in my love. If you keep my commandments, you will abide in my love, just as I have kept my Father's commandments and abide in his love. These things I have spoken to you, that my joy may be in you, and that your joy may be full.

"This is my commandment that you love one another as I have loved you."

*This lesson from the gospel shall be read,*

Matthew 19.4-6

Jesus said: "Have you not read that he who made them from the beginning made them male and female, and said, 'For this reason a man shall leave his father and mother and be joined to his wife, and the two shall become one'? So they are no longer two but one. What therefore God has joined together, let no man put asunder."

*The minister shall say to the people,*

We are gathered here in God's presence to witness the marriage of this man and woman, and to ask God to bless them. By our presence we accept responsibility for supporting them in the new relationship into which they are about to enter. We are called to rejoice in their happiness, to be patient when they make mistakes, to help them in times of trouble, and to remember them in our prayers.

God established marriage that man and woman might have life-long companionship, that natural instincts and affections might be fulfilled in mutual love, that children might have the benefit of family life, and that society might rest on a firm foundation. The apostle Paul compared married love to that of Christ for his church. Thus he gave us a new vision of what marriage ought to be, a life of self-giving love.

*And he shall say to the persons being married,*

Your marriage joins you for life in a relationship so intimate that it profoundly affects your whole being. It offers you the promise of a love that is true and mature. Such a love requires that you commit your lives to one another freely and without reserve, for the sake of a deeper and wider life together. Seek to become one in mind and heart as well as one in body. Trust in the living Christ, and he will guide and support you on your way.

*The minister shall say to the people,*
Let us pray for this man and woman as they make their marriage vows.

Almighty God who, from the beginning, hast made man and woman for each other: let thy Holy Spirit rest upon these thy servants, as in thy name they pledge themselves to one another in vows of love and faithfulness. Let thy love be upon them, as their hope is in thee; through Jesus Christ our Lord.
**Amen.**

*The minister may ask the people to stand. Then he shall say to the man,*
N. *Christian names,* Will you have this woman to be your wife?

*The man shall answer,*
I will.

*The minister shall say to the woman,*
N. *Christian names,* Will you have this man to be your husband?

*The woman shall answer,*
I will.

*The minister may say,*
Who gives this woman to be married to this man?

*The father, or whoever takes his place, shall answer,*
I do.

*The man and woman shall join their right hands, and the man shall say after the minister,*

In the presence of God and before these witnesses, I, N. *Christian names,* take you, N. *Christian names,* to be my wife, to have and to hold from this day forward, for better, for worse; for richer, for poorer; in sickness and in health; in joy and in sorrow; to love and to cherish and to be faithful to you alone, as long as we both shall live.

*And the woman shall say after the minister,*

In the presence of God and before these witnesses, I, N. *Christian names,* take you, N. *Christian names,* to be my husband, to have and to hold from this day forward, for better, for worse; for richer, for poorer; in sickness and in health; in joy and in sorrow; to love and to cherish and to be faithful to you alone, as long as we both shall live.

*A ring shall be given to the minister, and he shall give it to the man, who, placing it on the fourth finger of the woman's left hand, shall say after the minister,*

I give you this ring that you may wear it as a symbol of the vows we have made this day.

*If the woman gives the man a ring, the ceremony shall be repeated.*

*The minister shall say,*

Forasmuch as N. *Christian names and surname* and N. *Christian names and surname* have made this covenant of marriage before God and this company, I declare them to be husband and wife, in the name of the Father, and of the Son, and of the Holy Spirit.

*The man and woman may kiss one another.*

*And the minister shall pronounce this blessing upon them,*

The Lord bless and sustain you that you may please him in body and spirit, and grow together in love all the days of your life. **Amen.**

*The man and woman may kneel, the people may be seated, and the minister shall say,*

O God, Lord of life and Love eternal, Author of all good and Giver of all joy: we thank thee for the gift of marriage. We bless thee for the joy which these thy servants have found in each other, and for the covenant which they have made before thee.

Gracious Father, whose love is everlasting, grant that N. *Christian names* and N. *Christian names* may live together in unity and love all the days of their life. Give them health, prosperity and peace. Strengthen them to obey and serve thee, that they may walk in the steps of Jesus Christ thy Son. And when the joys and sorrows, and all the good and evil of this passing world are ended, let them inherit thy promises and share in thine eternal glory.

O God, our heavenly Father, look in favour upon all our homes. Defend them against evil from within and without, and supply their needs according to the riches of thy grace.

For ourselves also, we pray, O Lord, that directed by thy Spirit, we may look each to the good of others in word and deed, and grow in grace as we advance in years; through Jesus Christ our Lord.
**Amen.**

*And the Lord's Prayer shall be said by minister and people.*

**Our Father, who art in heaven,**
   **hallowed be thy name,**
      **thy kingdom come,**
      **thy will be done,**
         **on earth as it is in heaven.**
**Give us this day our daily bread,**
   **and forgive us our trespasses**
      **as we forgive those who trespass against us,**
      **and lead us not into temptation**
         **but deliver us from evil.**
**For thine is the kingdom, the power and the glory,**
      **for ever and ever. Amen.**

*The hymn* Saviour, who blessed the marriage feast, *or another suitable hymn such as* O perfect love, all human thought transcending, *or* Lead us, heavenly Father, lead us, *or* The Lord's my Shepherd, I'll not want, *may be sung.*

*The minister shall dismiss the people with a blessing.*

The grace of the Lord Jesus Christ and the love of God and the fellowship of the Holy Spirit be with you all. **Amen.**

*The marriage register shall be signed.*

*When the Lord's supper is to be celebrated at a wedding, the following emendations will be made: after the blessing of the man and the woman (page 199) a hymn shall be sung during which the elements shall be prepared; the prayers of thanksgiving, consecration and the Lord's Prayer customarily used as a celebration of the Lord's supper shall be said; when all have communicated the prayers, except the Lord's Prayer, hymn and blessing on page 199 shall follow.*

*When this order is used for the blessing of a civil marriage, the statement regarding intention and impediment (page 192) will be omitted and the address and prayer of invocation (pages 196-197) will be appropriately amended. The questions, vows and declaration will be replaced by the following,*

*The minister may ask the people to stand. Then he shall say to the man,*

N. *Christian names,* do you acknowledge this woman to be your wife, and before God do you promise to love her, to cherish her and to be faithful to her alone, as long as you both shall live?

*The man shall answer,*

I do.

*The minister shall say to the woman,*

N. *Christian names,* do you acknowledge this man to be your husband, and before God do you promise to love him, to cherish him and to be faithful to him alone, as long as you both shall live?

*The woman shall answer,*

I do.

*The minister shall pronounce this blessing upon them.*

The Lord bless and sustain you, that you may please him in body and spirit, and grow together in love all the days of your life. **Amen.**

*The minister shall continue as in the Solemnization of Marriage, page 199.*

## 2. THE BURIAL OF THE DEAD

AN OUTLINE FOR

**THE BURIAL OF THE DEAD**

Scripture Sentences
Hymn
Prayer of Approach
Lessons
Sermon
Prayers of Thanksgiving, Remembrance of the Departed,
    Intercession and Supplication
Lord's Prayer
Hymn
Blessing

*The Burial*     Scripture Sentences
Committal
Prayer of Supplication
Blessing

AN ORDER FOR

**THE BURIAL OF THE DEAD**

based on the foregoing outline

*This order may be used at the church, the house, or the funeral home. If there are two services, different sentences, prayers and scripture passages should be used at each.*

*Before the service begins the coffin shall be closed.*

*The minister shall say one or more of the following sentences,*

Jesus said, I am the resurrection and the life; he who believes in me, though he die, yet shall he live, and whoever lives and believes in me shall never die. *John 11. 25, 26*

The eternal God is your dwelling place, and underneath are the everlasting arms. *Deuteronomy 33. 27*

His favour is for a lifetime. Weeping may tarry for the night but joy comes with the morning.

*Psalm 30. 5*

God is our refuge and strength, a very present help in trouble. *Psalm 46. 1*

Cast your burden on the Lord, and he will sustain you. *Psalm 55. 22*

The Lord will not cast off for ever, but, though he cause grief, he will have compassion according to the abundance of his steadfast love.

*Lamentations 31. 32*

Blessed are those who mourn, for they shall be comforted. *Matthew 5. 4*

Let not your hearts be troubled; believe in God, believe also in me. In my Father's house are many rooms; if it were not so, would I have told you that I go to prepare a place for you?

*John 14. 1, 2*

I am sure that neither death, nor life, nor angels, nor principalities, nor things present, nor things to come, nor powers, nor height, nor depth, nor anything else in all creation, will be able to separate us from the love of God in Christ Jesus our Lord.

*Romans 8. 38, 39*

None of us lives to himself, and none of us dies to himself. If we live, we live to the Lord, and if we die, we die to the Lord; so then, whether we live or whether we die, we are the Lord's. For to this end Christ died and lived again, that he might be Lord both of the dead and of the living.

*Romans 14. 7-9*

I know whom I have believed and I am sure that he is able to guard until that Day what has been entrusted to me. *II Timothy 1. 12b*

Blessed be the God and Father of our Lord Jesus Christ! By his great mercy we have been born anew to a living hope through the resurrection of Jesus Christ from the dead and to an inheritance which is imperishable, undefiled, and unfading, kept in heaven for you. *I Peter 1. 3, 4*

*Then may be sung the hymn, O Lord of life, where'er they be, or other hymn setting forth the greatness and goodness of God, such as I'll praise my Maker, God is love, or Let Christian faith and hope dispel.*

*Then shall be said a prayer of approach.*

Eternal God, our heavenly Father, who lovest us with an everlasting love and canst turn the shadow of death into the light of a new day: help us now to wait upon thee with penitent and believing hearts, that, as we hear the words of eternal life, we may have hope, and be lifted above our present darkness and distress into the light and peace of thy presence; through Jesus Christ our Lord. **Amen.**

*Then shall be read some of the following lessons, including one or more of the psalms and one or more of the New Testament passages, the last of which shall be from the gospel.*

Psalm 23

The Lord is my shepherd, I shall not want; he makes me lie down in green pastures. He leads me beside still waters; he restores my soul. He leads me in paths of righteousness for his name's sake.

Even though I walk through the valley of the shadow of death, I fear no evil; for thou art with me; thy rod and thy staff, they comfort me.

Thou preparest a table before me in the presence of my enemies; thou anointest my head with oil, my cup overflows. Surely goodness and mercy shall follow me all the days of my life; and I shall dwell in the house of the Lord for ever.

Psalm 90. 1-6, 10, 12, 14-17

Lord, thou hast been our dwelling place in all generations. Before the mountains were brought forth, or ever thou hadst formed the earth and the world, from everlasting to everlasting thou art God.

Thou turnest man back to the dust and sayest, "Turn back, O children of men!" For a thousand years in thy sight are but as yesterday when it is past, or as a watch in the night.

Thou dost sweep men away; they are like a dream, like grass which is renewed in the morning: in the morning it flourishes and is renewed; in the evening it fades and withers.

The years of our life are threescore and ten, or even by reason of strength fourscore; yet their span is but toil and trouble; they are soon gone, and we fly away.

So teach us to number our days that we may get a heart of wisdom.

Satisfy us in the morning with thy steadfast love, that we may rejoice and be glad all our days. Make us glad as many days as thou hast afflicted us, and as many years as we have seen evil. Let thy work be manifest to thy servants, and thy glorious power to their children. Let the favour of the Lord our God be upon us, and establish thou the work of our hands upon us, yea, the work of our hands establish thou it.

Psalm 103. 13-17

As a father pities his children, so the Lord pities those who fear him. For he knows our frame; he remembers that we are dust.

As for man, his days are like grass; he flourishes like a flower of the field; for the wind passes over it, and it is gone, and its place knows it no more. But the steadfast love of the Lord is from ever-lasting to everlasting upon those who fear him, and his righteousness to children's children.

Psalm 116. 1-9

I love the Lord, because he has heard my voice and my supplications. Because he inclined his ear to me, therefore I will call on him as long as I live. The snares of death encompassed me; the pangs of Sheol laid hold on me; I suffered distress and anguish. Then I called on the name of the Lord "O Lord, I beseech thee, save my life!"

Gracious is the Lord, and righteous; our God is merciful. The Lord preserves the simple; when I was brought low, he saved me. Return, O my soul, to your rest; for the Lord has dealt bountifully with you.

For thou hast delivered my soul from death, my eyes from tears, my feet from stumbling; I walk before the Lord in the land of the living.

Psalm 121

I lift up my eyes to the hills. From whence does my help come? My help comes from the Lord, who made heaven and earth.

He will not let your foot be moved, he who keeps you will not slumber. Behold, he who keeps Israel will neither slumber nor sleep.

The Lord is your keeper; the Lord is your shade on your right hand. The sun shall not smite you by day, nor the moon by night.

The Lord will keep you from all evil; he will keep your life. The Lord will keep your going out and your coming in from this time forth and for ever-more.

## Psalm 130

Out of the depths I cry to thee, O Lord! Lord, hear my voice! Let thy ears be attentive to the voice of my supplications!

If thou, O Lord, shouldst mark iniquities, Lord, who could stand? But there is forgiveness with thee, that thou mayest be feared.

I wait for the Lord, my soul waits, and in his word I hope; my soul waits for the Lord more than watchmen for the morning, more than watch-men for the morning.

O Israel, hope in the Lord! For with the Lord there is steadfast love, and with him is plenteous redemption. And he will redeem Israel from all his iniquities.

## Psalm 139. 1-12, 17, 18

O Lord, thou hast searched me and known me! Thou knowest when I sit down and when I rise up! thou discernest my thoughts from afar. Thou searchest out my path and my lying down, and art acquainted with all my ways. Even before a word is on my tongue, lo, O Lord, thou knowest it altogether. Thou dost beset me behind and before, and layest thy hand upon me. Such knowledge is too wonderful for me: it is high, I cannot attain it.

Whither shall I go from thy Spirit? Or whither shall I flee from thy presence? If I ascend to heaven, thou art there! If I make my bed in Sheol, thou art there! If I take the wings of the morning and dwell in the uttermost parts of the sea, even there thy hand shall lead me, and thy right hand shall hold me. If I say, "Let only darkness cover me, and the light about me be night," even the darkness is not dark to thee, the night is bright as the day; for darkness is as light with thee.

How precious to me are thy thoughts, O God! How vast is the sum of them! If I would count them, they are more than the sand. When I awake, I am still with thee.

Wisdom 3. 1-3, 5; 5. 15.

The souls of the righteous are in the hand of God, and no torment will ever touch them. In the eyes of the foolish they seemed to have died, and their departure was thought to be an affliction, and their going from us to be their destruction; but they are at peace. Having been disciplined a little, they will receive great good, because God tested them and found them worthy of himself. Their reward is with the Lord; the most High takes care of them.

Romans 8. 18, 28, 35, 37-39

I consider that the sufferings of this present time are not worth comparing with the glory that is to be revealed to us.

We know that in everything God works for good with those who love him, who are called according to his purpose.

Who shall separate us from the love of Christ? Shall tribulation, or distress, or persecution, or famine, or nakedness, or peril, or sword? No, in all these things we are more than conquerors through him who loved us. For I am sure that neither death, nor life, nor angels, nor principalities, nor things present, nor things to come, nor powers, nor height, nor depth, nor anything else in all creation, will be able to separate us from the love of God in Christ Jesus our Lord.

I Corinthians 15. 20-22, 35-38, 42-44, 50, 53-58

Christ has been raised from the dead, the first fruits of those who have fallen asleep. For as by a man came death, by a man has come also the resurrection of the dead. For as in Adam all die, so also in Christ shall all be made alive.

But some one will ask, "How are the dead raised? With what kind of body do they come?" You foolish man! What you sow does not come to life unless it dies. And what you sow is not the body which is to be, but a bare kernel, perhaps of wheat or of some other grain. But God gives it a body as he has chosen, and to each kind of seed its own body.

So is it with the resurrection of the dead. What is sown is perishable, what is raised is imperishable. It is sown in dishonour, it is raised in glory. It is sown in weakness, it is raised in power. It is sown a physical body, it is raised a spiritual body. If there is a physical body, there is also a spiritual body. I tell you this, brethren: flesh and blood cannot inherit the kingdom of God, nor does the perishable inherit the imperishable.

For this perishable nature must put on the imperishable, and this mortal nature must put on immortality. When the perishable puts on the imperishable, and the mortal puts on immortality, then shall come to pass the saying that is written: "Death is swallowed up in victory."

"O death, where is thy victory?
O death, where is thy sting."

The sting of death is sin, and the power of sin is the law. But thanks be to God, who gives us the victory through our Lord Jesus Christ.

Therefore, my beloved brethren, be steadfast, immovable, always abounding in the work of the Lord, knowing that in the Lord your labour is not in vain.

II Corinthians 4. 8-18

We are afflicted in every way, but not crushed; perplexed, but not driven to despair; persecuted, but not forsaken; struck down, but not destroyed; always carrying in the body the death of Jesus, so that the life of Jesus may also be manifested in our bodies. For while we live we are always being given up to death for Jesus' sake, so that the life of Jesus may be manifested in our mortal flesh. So death is at work in us, but life in you.

Since we have the same spirit of faith as he had who wrote, "I believed, and so I spoke," we too believe, and so we speak, knowing that he who raised the Lord Jesus will raise us also with Jesus and bring us with you into his presence. For it is all for your sake, so that as grace extends to more and more people it may increase thanksgiving, to the glory of God.

So we do not lose heart. Though our outer nature is wasting away, our inner nature is being renewed every day. For this slight momentary affliction is preparing for us an eternal weight of glory beyond all comparison, because we look not to the things that are seen but to the things that are unseen; for the things that are seen are transient, but the things that are unseen are eternal.

Revelation 7. 9-17

After this I looked, and behold, a great multitude which no man could number, from every nation, from all tribes and peoples and tongues, standing before the throne and before the Lamb, clothed in white robes, with palm branches in their hands, and crying out with a loud voice, "Salvation belongs to our God who sits upon the throne, and to the Lamb!" And all the angels stood round the throne and round the elders and the four living creatures, and they fell on their faces before the throne and worshipped God, saying, "Amen! Blessing and glory and wisdom and thanksgiving and honour and power and might be to our God for ever and ever! Amen."

Then one of the elders addressed me, saying, "Who are these, clothed in white robes, and whence have they come?" I said to him, "Sir, you know." And he said to me, "These are they who have come out of the great tribulation; they have washed their robes and made them white in the blood of the Lamb.

Therefore are they before the throne of God, and serve him day and night within his temple; and he who sits upon the throne will shelter them with his presence.

They shall hunger no more, neither thirst any more; the sun shall not strike them, nor any scorching heat.

For the Lamb in the midst of the throne will be their shepherd, and he will guide them to springs of living water; and God will wipe away every tear from their eyes."

Revelation 21. 1-4

Then I saw a new heaven and a new earth; for the first heaven and the first earth had passed away, and the sea was no more. And I saw the holy city, new Jerusalem, coming down out of heaven from God, prepared as a bride adorned for her husband; and I heard a great voice from the throne saying, "Behold, the dwelling of God is with men. He will dwell with them, and they shall be his people, and God himself will be with them; he will wipe away every tear from their eyes, and death shall be no more, neither shall there be mourning nor crying nor pain any more, for the former things have passed away."

Revelation 22. 1-5

Then he showed me the river of the water of life, bright as crystal, flowing from the throne of God and of the Lamb through the middle of the street of the city; also, on either side of the river, the tree of life with its twelve kinds of fruit, yielding its fruit each month; and the leaves of the tree were for the healing of the nations. There shall no more be anything accursed, but the throne of God and of the Lamb shall be in it, and his servants shall worship him; they shall see his face, and his name shall be on their foreheads. And night shall be no more; they need no light of lamp or sun, for the Lord God will be their light, and they shall reign for ever and ever.

John 6. 37-40

Jesus said to them, "All that the Father gives me will come to me; and him who comes to me I will not cast out. For I have come down from heaven, not to do my own will, but the will of him who sent me; and this is the will of him who sent me, that I should lose nothing of all that he has given me, but raise it up at the last day. For this is the will of my Father, that every one who sees the Son and believes in him should have eternal life; and I will raise him up at the last day."

## John 11. 21-26a

Martha said to Jesus, "Lord, if you had been here, my brother would not have died. And even now I know that whatever you ask from God, God will give you." Jesus said to her, "Your brother will rise again." Martha said to him, "I know that he will rise again in the resurrection at the last day." Jesus said to her, "I am the resurrection and the life; he who believes in me, though he die, yet shall he live, and whoever lives and believes in me shall never die."

## John 14. 1-6, 18, 19, 27

Jesus said, "Let not your hearts be troubled; believe in God, believe also in me. In my Father's house are many rooms; if it were not so, would I have told you that I go to prepare a place for you? And when I go and prepare a place for you, I will come again and will take you to myself, that where I am you may be also. And you know the way where I am going." Thomas said to him, "Lord, we do not know where you are going; how can we know the way?" Jesus said to him, "I am the way, and the truth, and the life; no one comes to the Father, but by me."

"I will not leave you desolate; I will come to you. Yet a little while, and the world will see me no more, but you will see me; because I live, you will live also."

"Peace I leave with you; my peace I give to you; not as the world gives do I give to you. Let not your hearts be troubled, neither let them be afraid."

*A sermon may be preached declaring the love of God in the redemption of man by Christ Jesus.*

*The minister shall then lead the congregation in prayers of thanksgiving, remembrance of the departed, intercession and supplication. Prayers which may be used in specially distressing circumstances are found on pages 221-222.*

All glory and thanksgiving be to thee, almighty God, our heavenly Father, that thou of thy tender mercy didst give thine only Son Jesus Christ to take our nature upon him, to suffer death upon the cross for our redemption and to rise victorious over sin and death. Therefore, with all creation and with all the company of the redeemed, we magnify thy glorious name; evermore praising thee and saying,

**Holy, holy, holy, Lord God of hosts,**
  **heaven and earth are full of thy glory.**
**Glory be to thee, O Lord most high.**

O God, with whom do live the souls of the righteous: we praise thee for the great cloud of witnesses by whom we are surrounded, thy saints in every age who have loved thee in life, and continued faithful unto death, thy servants who have departed in the faith and are at rest with thee. Especially do we bless thee for  N. *Christian names and surname* whom we now remember before thee. For all thy loving kindness towards *him* throughout his earthly life, and all thou hast accomplished through *him,* we give thee thanks.

*Here may be made particular reference to the departed.*

And since in Christ thou has provided an inheritance imperishable, undefiled and unfading, we thank thee that, for thy servants who have departed from this life, death itself is past and they have entered into the joy of their Lord.

O merciful God, the consolation of the sorrowful and the support of the weary: look down in tender love and pity upon thy servants whose joy is turned into mourning; so that, while they mourn, they may not lose heart or abandon faith but remembering all thy mercies, thy promises, and thy love in Christ, may yield themselves into thy hands, to be taught and sustained by thee. Fill their hearts with thy love, that they may hold fast to thee, who bringest life out of death, and who canst turn their grief into eternal joy.

O Lord God, who knowest the way that we must go: guide us on our journey and grant that we, who have stood in the presence of death, may at all times remember that we stand also in the presence of him who is alive for evermore. Give us such faith in his saving power that, being upheld by his love and faithfulness, we may be enabled to run with perseverance the race that is set before us and, in thine own time and in thy great mercy, may be brought to the glory of thine eternal kingdom.

O Lord, support us all the day long of this troublous life, until the shadows lengthen and the evening comes, and the busy world is hushed, and the fever of life is over, and our work is done. Then of thy tender mercy grant us a safe lodging, and a holy rest, and peace at the last; through Jesus Christ our Lord. **Amen.**

*The Lord's Prayer shall be said by minister and people.*

*Then may be sung* Now thank we all our God, *or* O thou my soul, bless God the Lord, *or* Blest be the everlasting God *or another hymn declaring victory over death.*

*Then shall the minister dismiss the people with a blessing.*

The peace of God, which passeth all understanding, keep your hearts and minds in the knowledge and love of God, and of his Son Jesus Christ our Lord: and the blessing of God almighty, the Father, the Son and the Holy Spirit, be upon you and remain with you always. **Amen.**

## THE BURIAL

*When all are assembled at the grave, the minister shall say these sentences from Holy Scripture.*

God is our refuge and strength, a very present help in trouble. Therefore we will not fear.　　*Psalm 46. 1*

Thanks be to God, who gives us the victory through our Lord Jesus Christ. Therefore, my beloved brethren, be steadfast, immovable, always abounding in the work of the Lord, knowing that in the Lord your labour is not in vain.

*I Corinthians 15. 57, 58*

Jesus said, I am the resurrection and the life; he who believes in me, though he die, yet shall he live, and whoever lives and believes in me shall never die.　　*John 11. 25, 26*

*He may add one or more of the following.*

As a father pities his children, so the Lord pities those who fear him. For he knows our frame; he remembers that we are dust. As for man, his days are like grass; he flourishes like a flower of the field; for the wind passes over it, and it is gone, and its place knows it no more.
But the steadfast love of the Lord is from everlasting to everlasting upon those who fear him, and his righteousness to children's children.

*Psalm 103. 13-17*

Fear not, I am the first and the last, and the living one; I died, and behold I am alive for evermore, and I have the keys of Death and Hades.

*Revelation 1. 17, 18*

They shall hunger no more, neither thirst any more; the sun shall not strike them, nor any scorching heat. For the Lamb in the midst of the throne will be their shepherd, and he will guide them to springs of living water; and God will wipe away every tear from their eyes.

*Revelation 7. 17, 18*

*Earth may be cast upon the coffin, and the minister shall say,*

Into God's keeping we commend our *brother* here departed. We commit *his* body to the ground; earth to earth, ashes to ashes, dust to dust; trusting in God's great mercy by which we have been born anew to a living hope through the resurrection of Jesus Christ from the dead.

*At the burial of the dead at sea, instead of the words,* we commit his body to the ground, *may be said,* we commit *his* body to the deep, looking for the resurrection of the dead and the life of the world to come, through our Lord Jesus Christ.

*At a cremation, instead of the words, his* body to the ground, *may be said, his* body to the elements.

*At the burial of the ashes after cremation, instead of the words, his* body to the ground . . . dust to dust, *may be said, his* ashes to the ground, earth to earth, dust to dust.

*Then may be said,*

I heard a voice from heaven saying, Blessed are the dead who die in the Lord henceforth. Blessed indeed, says the Spirit, that they may rest from their labours, for their deeds follow them.

*Revelation 14. 13*

*Then shall follow a prayer of supplication.*

O God, whose days are without end, and whose mercies cannot be numbered: make us deeply sensitive to the shortness and uncertainty of human life, and let thy Holy Spirit lead us through this present world in holiness and righteousness all the days of our life; that, when we have served thee in our day and generation, we may be received by thee, our Father, having the testimony of a good conscience, in the communion of thy church, in the confidence of a certain faith, in the comfort of a holy hope, in favour with thee, our God, and in perfect charity with all mankind; through Jesus Christ our Lord. **Amen.**

*Then shall the minister dismiss the people with a blessing.*

Now may the God of peace who brought again from the dead our Lord Jesus, that great shepherd of the sheep, by the blood of the everlasting covenant, equip you with everything good that you may do his will, working in you that which is pleasing in his sight, through Jesus Christ; to whom be glory for ever and ever. **Amen.**

### Prayers which May Be Used in Specially Distressing Circumstances

*In the service for the burial of the dead, the prayers below may be used instead of those beginning,* O God, with whom do live the souls of the righteous *and* O Merciful God, the consolation of the sorrowful.

Gracious God, who in thy love hast fathomed the depth of human suffering in the cross of Jesus Christ and who in all our afflictions art afflicted: to thy fatherly care we commend *him* who has been overcome by the chaos of the world without and the agony of the soul within. Where wrong has been done, where responsibility has been evaded and where the ties of affection have been broken, we pray that in thy mercy thou wilt judge and in thy love forgive. **Amen.**

Eternal Father, whose compassion is infinite: comfort, we pray thee, thy servants unto whom this trial has come. Be thou their stay, their strength and their shield. Grant that, trusting in thee to lighten their darkness and to bring them out of all their distress, they may be delivered from all bitterness, despair and doubt. Touch our hearts with thy love in this hour, that the springs of compassion may flow. Grant us grace to help and comfort those who find themselves desolate and lead us with them in the paths of quietness and hope; through Jesus Christ our Lord. **Amen.**

# 3. THE BURIAL OF A CHILD

AN OUTLINE FOR

## THE BURIAL OF A CHILD

Scripture Sentences
Prayer of Approach
Psalm
Lessons
Sermon
Prayers of Thanksgiving, Remembrance of the Departed
    and Intercession
Lord's Prayer
Hymn
Blessing

*The Burial*    Scripture Sentences
Committal
Prayer of Intercession
Blessing

AN ORDER FOR

## THE BURIAL OF A CHILD

based on the foregoing outline

*This order may be used at the church, the house or the funeral home.*

*Before the service begins the coffin shall be closed.*

*The minister shall say one or more of the following sentences.*

Wait for the Lord; be strong, and let your heart take courage; yea, wait for the Lord.     *Psalm 27. 14*

As a father pities his children, so the Lord pities those who fear him.     *Psalm 103. 13*

He will feed his flock like a shepherd, he will gather the lambs in his arms, he will carry them in his bosom.     *Isaiah 40. 11*

As one whom his mother comforts, so I will comfort you, says the Lord.     *Isaiah 66. 13*

Blessed are those who mourn, for they shall be comforted.     *Matthew 5. 4*

Let the children come to me, do not hinder them; for to such belongs the kingdom of God.

*Mark 10. 14*

Let not your hearts be troubled; believe in God, believe also in me.     *John 14. 1*

*Then shall be said a prayer of approach.*

Most loving Father, whose ear is ever open to the cry of thy children, and who art a very present help in time of trouble: unto thee do we turn in this hour of sorrow, knowing thy love to us, and trusting in thy perfect wisdom; through Jesus Christ our Lord. **Amen.**

*Then shall Psalm 23 be sung or said.*

*Then two or more of the following lessons shall be read, the last of which shall be from the gospel.*

## Romans 8. 35, 37-39

Who shall separate us from the love of Christ? Shall tribulation, or distress, or persecution, or famine, or nakedness, or peril, or sword? No, in all these things we are more than conquerors through him who loved us. For I am sure that neither death, nor life, nor angels, nor principalities, nor things present, nor things to come, nor powers, nor height, nor depth, nor anything else in all creation, will be able to separate us from the love of God in Christ Jesus our Lord.

## Matthew 18. 1-5, 10-14

At that time the disciples came to Jesus, saying, "Who is the greatest in the kingdom of heaven?" And calling to him a child, he put him in the midst of them, and said, "Truly, I say to you, unless you turn and become like children, you will never enter the kingdom of heaven. Whoever humbles himself like this child, he is the greatest in the kingdom of heaven. Whoever receives one such child in my name receives me.

"See that you do not despise one of these little ones; for I tell you that in heaven their angels always behold the face of my Father who is in heaven. What do you think? If a man has a hundred sheep, and one of them has gone astray, does he not leave the ninety-nine on the hills and go in search of the one that went astray? And if he finds it, truly, I say to you, he rejoices over it more than over the ninety-nine that never went astray. So it is not the will of my Father who is in heaven that one of these little ones should perish.''

Mark 10. 13-16

They were bringing children to Jesus, that he might touch them; and the disciples rebuked them. But when Jesus saw it he was indignant, and said to them, "Let the children come to me, do not hinder them; for to such belongs the kingdom of God. Truly, I say to you, whoever does not receive the kingdom of God like a child shall not enter it." And he took them in his arms and blessed them, laying his hands upon them.

John 14. 1-6, 18, 19, 27

Jesus said, "Let not your hearts be troubled; believe in God, believe also in me. In my Father's house are many rooms; if it were not so, would I have told you that I go to prepare a place for you? And when I go and prepare a place for you, I will come again and will take you to myself, that where I am you may be also. And you know the way where I am going." Thomas said to him, "Lord, we do not know where you are going; how can we know the way?" Jesus said to him, "I am the way, and the truth, and the life; no one comes to the Father, but by me.

"I will not leave you desolate; I will come to you. Yet a little while, and the world will see me no more, but you will see me; because I live, you will live also.

"Peace I leave with you; my peace I give to you; not as the world gives do I give to you. Let not your hearts be troubled, neither let them be afraid."

*A sermon may be preached declaring the love of God in the redemption of man by Christ Jesus.*

*Then shall be said prayers of thanksgiving and intercession.*

Let us give thanks to God for his mighty acts.

All glory and thanksgiving be to thee, almighty God, our heavenly Father, that thou didst create man in thine own image and that thou of thy tender mercy didst give thine only Son Jesus Christ to take our nature upon him, to suffer death upon the cross for our redemption and to rise victorious over sin and death. Therefore, with angels and archangels, and with all the company of heaven, we laud and magnify thy glorious name; evermore praising thee and saying,

**Holy, holy, holy, Lord God of hosts,**
**heaven and earth are full of thy glory.**
**Glory be to thee, O Lord most high.**

Let us thank God for his love in giving and receiving this child.

Heavenly Father, whose Son Jesus Christ did take little children into his arms and bless them: we thank thee that thou didst give this child to us, and cause our hearts to love *him,* and thy church to cherish *him.* We praise and bless thee for the assurance that thou hast received *him* unto thyself, and that thou wilt keep him now and always in the arms of thy mercy; through the same Jesus Christ our Lord. **Amen.**

Let us pray for those who mourn.

O God, our heavenly Father, whose tender mercies are over all thy works and whose compassion never fails: we commend to thee those who mourn. Grant unto them thy strength and consolation that they may be upheld by a living hope. May the words of thy Son our Saviour, which reveal his love for little children, speak peace to their troubled hearts. Make them to know that the child who has been taken out of their sight is with thee, safe in thine eternal care, and that in thine own good time they will see him again; through Jesus Christ our Lord. **Amen.**

*The Lord's Prayer shall be said by minister and people.*

*Then may be sung the hymn,* I to the hills will lift mine eyes, or O Lord of Life, where'er they be.

*Then shall the minister dismiss the people with a blessing.*

The peace of God which passeth all understanding, keep your hearts and minds in the knowledge and love of God, and of his Son Jesus Christ our Lord; and the blessing of God almighty, the Father, the Son, and the Holy Spirit, be amongst you and remain with you always. **Amen.**

### THE BURIAL

*When all are assembled at the grave, the minister shall say one or more of these sentences from Holy Scripture.*

The eternal God is your dwelling place and underneath are the everlasting arms. *Deuteronomy 33. 37*

As a father pities his children, so the Lord pities those who fear him. *Psalm 103. 13*

Jesus said, "Let the children come to me, do not hinder them; for to such belongs the kingdom of God." *Mark 10. 14*

They shall hunger no more, neither thirst any more; the sun shall not strike them, nor any scorching heat. For the Lamb in the midst of the throne will be their shepherd, and he will guide them to springs of living water; and God will wipe away every tear from their eyes. *Revelation 7. 16, 17*

*Then shall be said words of committal.*

In the faith of our Lord Jesus Christ, who took little children in his arms and blessed them, we commit to the ground the body of this child in the assurance that *he* lives in the glory of God's presence and that *he* is safe in his holy keeping for evermore.

*At a cremation, instead of the words,* we commit to the ground the body of this child *may be said,* we commit the body of this child to the elements.

*At the burial of the ashes after cremation, instead of the word* body *the word* ashes *may be used.*

*Then shall follow a prayer of intercession.*

O God, who makest nothing in vain, and who lovest all that thou hast made: comfort thy servants in their great sorrow; and grant that they may so love and serve thee in this life, that together with this thy child, they may obtain the fulness of thy promises in the world to come; through Jesus Christ our Lord. **Amen.**

*Then shall follow this blessing.*

Now may the God of peace who brought again from the dead our Lord Jesus, the great shepherd of the sheep, through the blood of the eternal covenant, equip you with everything good that you may do his will, working in you that which is pleasing in his sight, through Jesus Christ; to whom be glory for ever and ever. **Amen.**

# 4. THE WELCOMING OF MEMBERS

## Introduction

Persons are admitted to full membership by action of the session a) by certificate "in good standing" from other United Church congregations; b) by certificate "in good standing" from other churches holding the reformed tradition; c) when unable to obtain a certificate (for example, Anglican, Lutheran, Roman Catholic) upon clear assurance that they have been baptized and confirmed, and, where necessary, after instruction in the practice and doctrine of the United Church. (Manual #13)

This service is an act of public worship by which the congregation welcomes into its fellowship those who have been admitted by the session. Even if a person is not able to be present at the welcoming, the action of the session adds his name to the roll.

AN ORDER FOR
## THE WELCOMING OF MEMBERS
## FROM OTHER CHURCHES

For use in a service of public worship

*The session, having fulfilled the requirements of the Manual concerning the transfer, restoration, instruction, or reaffirmation of members, and having taken action to admit them to full membership in the congregation, may present them to be welcomed at a service of public worship. This order is not, at any time, to be used as a substitute for confirmation*

*Following the sermon, the minister shall say to the people,*

A Christian is a member of the holy catholic church. He exercises this membership in the denomination to which he belongs, which for us is The United Church of Canada, and within the fellowship of a local congregation.

We are now to welcome into this congregation persons who are already members of the church of our Lord Jesus Christ.

*The clerk of session shall summon by name the new members, and he shall say to the minister,*

Sir, the session has made inquiry concerning these persons, and has admitted them to full membership in this congregation of The United Church of Canada.

*The minister shall say to the people,*

Let us rise to receive these new members.

*Minister.*

In the name of the Lord Jesus Christ we welcome you to the privileges and responsibilities of membership in this congregation.

As God has called you, live up to your calling.

As God's children, try to be like him, and live in love as Christ loves you.

Be generous to one another, tender-hearted, forgiving one another as God in Christ forgave you. Whatever you are doing, whether you speak or act, do everything in the name of the Lord Jesus, giving thanks to God the Father through him.

*People.*

**As God has called us, we pledge to you our friendship, our help and our prayers.**

*The minister shall say a suitable blessing.*

May the almighty God order your days in his peace, and grant you his blessing. **Amen.**

*The minister and clerk of session shall extend to the new members the right hand of fellowship. All shall return to their places and the order of worship shall be resumed.*

# 5. THE RESTORATION OF MEMBERS

## Introduction

Persons whose names have been removed from the roll by action of the session or whose certificates are not "in good standing" (Manual #16, #13(c)) are restored or admitted by action of the session on reaffirmation of faith

This service shall normally be held within the session. The Committee on Christian Faith recommends that reaffirmation can best be made in the presence of the session.

Persons restored or admitted to full membership by action of the session should then be welcomed into the congregation during public worship using an Order for the Welcoming of Members from Other Churches.

AN ORDER FOR
## THE RESTORATION OR ADMISSION OF MEMBERS
## ON REAFFIRMATION OF FAITH

*This order shall be used when the persons desiring to be restored or admitted to full membership are required by the Manual to make a reaffirmation of faith. This order is not, at any time, to be used as a substitute for confirmation.*

*At the time appointed, the minister shall say,*

It is the duty of the session to keep the roll of church members, to admit persons to full membership, to grant certificates of removal, to exercise discipline, and to restore to full communion those who make an acceptable reaffirmation of faith.

The session must always seek to exercise this solemn duty under the guidance of the Holy Spirit, in order that God's will may be done among us.

*A prayer of confession shall be said by minister and people. The minister shall give an assurance of pardon.*

Here are words you may trust, words that merit full acceptance: Christ Jesus came into the world to save sinners.

Accept God's pardon and be assured that his grace is all you need.

*The clerk of session shall summon by name the persons who are being restored or admitted to membership, and he shall say to the minister,*

Sir, the session has made inquiry concerning these persons, and recommends that they be restored (*or* admitted) to full membership in The United Church of Canada, and within this congregation.

*The minister shall say to them,*

By baptism you were made members of the church of Jesus Christ and were adopted into the family and household of God. On profession of your Christian faith you were confirmed, or otherwise received into the full communion of your church. You desire now to be restored (*or* admitted) to full membership in The United Church of Canada, and within this congregation. I ask you, therefore, before God and these people,

Do you profess anew your faith in God your heavenly Father, in Jesus Christ your Saviour and Lord, and in the Holy Spirit your Teacher and Guide?

*Answer.*

I do.

Do you reaffirm your solemn intention to join with the Lord's people to worship him, to study the Bible and to pray; to enter into the life and work of the church, supporting it with your gifts, and sharing in its mission to all men; daily to respond to God's love, to do his will, and to fulfil your Christian calling and ministry in the world?

*Answer.*

I do, God being my helper.

*When circumstances make it desirable the minister shall say,*

Are you in essential agreement with the practice and doctrine of The United Church of Canada, and are you willing to submit to its lawful discipline?

*Answer.*

I am, God being my helper.

*The minister shall say,*

In the name of the Lord Jesus Christ, and by authority of the session of ............. United Church, I restore (*or* admit) you to full membership in The United Church of Canada within this congregation.

*Prayers of thanksgiving, intercession and supplication shall follow.*

Almighty God, who, in thy wisdom and power, dost make all things new, confirming thy promises and renewing our hopes: we thank thee that these thy servants have been moved to declare the faith that thy Spirit has rekindled within them.

Give them a vision of thy holy purpose; re-enlist them in the service of thy kingdom; and make them loyal and courageous soldiers of Christ the Lord.

Renew a right spirit within us, and restore to us the joy of thy salvation. Surround us with thy love and mercy, that we may always know the peace of thy presence.

Guide us safely through the perils of temptation, and bring us at last to our heavenly inheritance in the fellowship of the church and the company of the redeemed; through Jesus Christ our Lord. **Amen.**

The Lord's Prayer shall be said by minister and people.

And the minister shall say a suitable blessing.

The minister and clerk of session shall extend to the new members the right hand of fellowship.

These new members may be welcomed thereafter, in company with persons who have transferred by certificate, at a service of public worship according to an Order for the Welcoming of Members from Other Churches.

## 6. THE RECEPTION OF AN ASSISTANT
## TO THE MINISTER

### Introduction

This order may be used in the case of the appointment by a congregation of an assistant to the minister. Such an assistant may be a retired minister, a minister of another communion serving within the United Church, a minister on leave of absence, or a lay assistant. Special orders are provided for presbyteries in the case of an additional minister, a deaconess, and a certified employed churchman.

AN ORDER FOR
**THE RECEPTION OF**
**AN ASSISTANT TO THE MINISTER**

*The service shall begin with THE APPROACH and THE WORD OF GOD as in the First Order for Public Worship. It shall then proceed as follows,*

**The Response**

*The offerings of the people shall be collected and presented. An offertory prayer shall be said.*
*A hymn appropriate to the occasion shall be sung.*
*The recording steward shall present the person to be received to the minister and shall say.*

Sir, I present to you N. *Christian names and surname* who has been invited by the congregation to be assistant to the minister.

*The minister shall read one or more of the following lessons.*
John 21. 15-17

Jesus said to Simon Peter, "Simon, son of John, do you love me more than these?" He said to him, "Yes, Lord; you know that I love you." He said to him, "Feed my lambs." A second time he said to him, "Simon, son of John, do you love me?" He said to him. "Yes, Lord; you know that I love you." He said to him, "Tend my sheep." He said to him the third time, "Simon, son of John, do you love me?" Peter was grieved because he said to him the third time, "Do you love me?" And he said to him, "Lord, you know everything; you know that I love you." Jesus said to him, "Feed my sheep."

Ephesians 4. 7, 11-13

Grace was given to each of us according to the measure of Christ's gift. And his gifts were that some should be apostles, some prophets, some evangelists, some pastors and teachers, for the equipment of the saints, for the work of the ministry, for building up of the body of Christ, until we all attain to the unity of the faith and of the knowledge of the Son of God, to mature manhood, to the measure of the stature of the fulness of Christ.

I Peter 5, 1-4

I exhort the elders among you, as a fellow elder and a witness of the sufferings of Christ as well as a partaker in the glory that is to be revealed. Tend the flock of God that is your charge, not by constraint but willingly, not for shameful gain but eagerly, not as domineering over those in your charge but being examples to the flock, and when the chief Shepherd is manifested you will obtain the unfading crown of glory.

*The minister shall say to the assistant,*
My *brother* in Christ,

do you accept the office of assistant to the minister, and do you promise to perform faithfully the duties of your ministry in this congregation?

*Answer.*

I do so promise, God being my helper.

*The minister shall say to the people,*

You have heard the promise of *him* whom you have invited to be assistant to the minister. I ask you, therefore, do you receive N. *Christian names and surname,* and do you promise to support his ministry?

*The people shall rise in assent.*

*The ministers and people shall say,*

**Almighty God, who hast heard the promises we have made, grant us grace to keep them and to continue in every good work; through Jesus Christ our Lord. Amen.**

*The minister shall say,*

In the name of the Lord Jesus Christ, the King and Head of the Church, we welcome you as assistant to the minister in this congregation. The blessing of God almighty, Father, Son and Holy Spirit, rest upon and remain with you always.

*The minister and the recording steward shall extend the right hand of fellowship.*

*The people shall be seated. Then shall follow prayers of thanksgiving and intercession.*

*Minister.*

Let us give thanks to God.

For thy Son sent into the world to reveal thy glory; for his life and example, his sacrifice on the cross, his rising again in power, his glorious ascension, and his presence in our midst through the Holy Spirit; with all our heart and mind,

*People.*

**We thank thee, Lord.**

*Minister.*

For the church he founded, for the faithful witnesses through whom the gospel has been made known to us, and for our fellowship with thee and with one another; with all our heart and mind,

*People.*

**We thank thee, Lord.**

*Minister.*

For all who have fought the good fight of faith and have entered into their rest, and especially those whom we have known and loved who have passed from this earthly fellowship into the joy of thy presence; with all our heart and mind,

*People.*

**We thank thee, Lord.**

*Minister.*

Let us make our intercessions to the Lord our God. We pray that thy church may be true to the mission given to it by thy Son: that it may be one as thou art one, and by word and deed proclaim the gospel of thy love. Lord, hear our prayer:

*People.*

**And in thy love answer us.**

*Minister.*

We pray for thy servant   N. *Christian names and surname* appointed to minister in this congregation. Direct *him* by thy Holy Spirit, give *him* zeal in the service of thy kingdom, and renew *him* in faith, hope and love. Let the mind of Christ ever rule *him* and dwell in *him*. Lord, hear our prayer:

*People.*
**And in thy love answer us.**

*Minister.*
We pray for all who lead and teach. Endow them with the gifts they need; keep them faithful in their work; hallow their love and service and deepen their knowledge of the truth as it is in Jesus Christ. Lord, hear our prayer:

*People.*
**And in thy love answer us.**

*Minister.*
We pray for all who are in trouble, sorrow, sickness, need or any other trial, that thy comfort and strength may be theirs. Lord, hear our prayer:

*People.*
**And in thy love answer us.**

*Minister and people.*
**O God our Father, who hast called us to be thy servant people, grant that we may live in thy spirit and love each other as Christ has loved us. Amen.**

*The Lord's Prayer shall be said by minister and people.*

*A hymn may be sung.*

*The minister shall commission the people.*

Go into the world in the power of the Holy Spirit to fulfil your high calling as servants and soldiers of Jesus Christ.

*And he shall dismiss them with a blessing.*

The grace of the Lord Jesus Christ, and the love of God, and the fellowship of the Holy Spirit, be with you all. **Amen.**

# 7. THE INDUCTION OF ELDERS

AN ORDER FOR
**THE INDUCTION OF ELDERS**

Members of Session are called Elders

*The service shall begin with THE APPROACH and THE WORD OF GOD as in the First Order for Public Worship. It shall then proceed as follows,*

**The Response**

*The offerings of the people shall be collected and presented.*

*An offertory prayer shall be said.*

*A hymn appropriate to the occasion shall be sung.*

*The clerk of session shall present the elders-elect, saying,*

Sir, I present to you the following persons who have been elected to the session by this congregation.

*Here he shall read their names and they shall come forward.*

*The minister shall address them, saying,*

You have been called by the grace of God, and duly elected by this congregation, to be an elder of ......................... United Church.

It is the duty and privilege of a member of session to share with the minister in the government and pastoral oversight of the congregation. The session has responsibility for worship in the church, for the administration of the sacraments, for the Christian training of the people, for keeping the roll of membership, and for the outreach of the congregation in the community and the world.

As you come now to assume the duties of your office, I ask you before God and this congregation, Do you profess your faith in God your heavenly Father, in Jesus Christ your Saviour and Lord, and in the Holy Spirit your Teacher and Guide?

*Answer.*

I do.

Will you endeavour to carry out your responsibilities in this congregation with integrity and devotion?

*Answer.*

I will, God being my helper.

*The elders-elect may kneel, and the minister shall say,*

Let us, in silence, pray for these men and women.

*After a period of silence, the minister shall pray, saying,*

Almighty God, grant thy Holy Spirit to these men and women, that they may be enabled to keep the promises they have made before thee, and may fulfil with wisdom and compassion the duties to which they are called by thy grace; through Jesus Christ our Lord. **Amen.**

*The elders-elect shall stand and the minister, taking each in turn by the right hand, shall say to him*

N. *Christian names and surname,* in the name of the Lord Jesus Christ, I induct you an elder of this congregation.
Go and minister in Christ's name among these people, and serve him faithfully in the world.

*After the minister has inducted them all, the clerk and one or more of the other members of session shall extend the right hand of fellowship to them.*

*The elders shall be seated*

*Prayers of thanksgiving and intercession shall follow.*

Almighty God, who makest all things new, we praise thee for Jesus Christ thy Son our Saviour. We bless thee for the church he founded, for the diversities of the gifts of his Spirit, and for all those who have borne witness to his redeeming truth and love.

We thank thee for these thy servants who today have answered thy call to serve on the session of this congregation.

Almighty God, who hast called the church out of the world that she may bring the world to thee, we pray for this congregation and especially for the elders. Grant that they may ever be ministers of thy comfort and heralds of thy hope.

Merciful Father, whose compassion fails not, sustain and encourage those who struggle for freedom, and shelter those who have no protector. Lift up the fallen, relieve the suffering, feed the hungry and give thy peace to the dying.

O God, without whose aid we can do nothing, we pray for ourselves. Give success to our labours and show us how we may serve thee better in the community and the world. Strengthen us to follow wherever thy love calls us to go.

And to thee shall be the glory. **Amen.**

*The Lord's Prayer shall be said by minister and people.*
*The service shall proceed to its conclusion.*

# 8. THE INSTALLATION OF TEACHERS, OFFICERS AND LEADERS

AN ORDER FOR
**THE INSTALLATION OF TEACHERS,
OFFICERS AND LEADERS**

*This order may be used for the installation of members of
the Committee of Stewards, church school teachers and
officers, officers of the United Church Men or Women, and
mid-week leaders.*

*If this order is used in public worship it should immediately
precede the offering.*

*At the appropriate time, the clerk of session or a representa-
tive of the organization shall read the names of the persons
to be installed and they shall come forward.*

*The minister shall read a suitable passage from Scripture.*

Romans 12. 6-10a

The gifts we possess differ as they are allotted to
us by God's grace, and must be exercised accordingly: the gift of inspired utterance, for example,
in proportion to a man's faith; or the gift of administration, in administration. A teacher should em-
ploy his gift in teaching, and one who has the gift
of stirring speech should use it to stir his hearers.
If you give to charity, give with all your heart; if
you are a leader, exert yourself to lead; if you are
helping others in distress, do it cheerfully.

Love in all sincerity, loathing evil and clinging to
the good. Let love for our brotherhood breed
warmth of mutual affection.

*Then the minister shall say,*

Each of us is called by God to fulfil a ministry in
the world. We are also called to offer such gifts as
we are able within the church so that it may more

effectively fulfil its ministry of worship, witness and work. You are now offering *yourselves* for service in this congregation of the church through the *(name of organization or office)*.

In the exercise of your responsibilities you will need to continue to study and grow in the faith. Be diligent in your work, confident that this community of Christ will support you in love.

The power of Christ is adequate for each of us.

*Minister.*

Will you accept the responsibilities of this office in the church?

*Answer.*

I will, the Lord being my helper.

*Minister.*

Will you seek, through your office, to make the witness of this congregation more effective in the world?

*Answer.*

I will, the Lord being my helper.

*Then the minister shall say one of the following prayers,*

**For Teachers and Officers of the Church School**

Eternal God, who dost call us into thy service and dost promise grace and strength for the fulfilling of thy will, bless, we pray thee, these *teachers and officers* who have offered themselves for work in this church school. Lead them to a deeper knowledge of thee. Give them diligence and faithfulness in their study of thy word, tenderness and patience with children and youth. Help us all so to follow Christ that his will may at length be done on earth as in heaven; who with thee, and the Holy Spirit, ever livest and reignest one God, world without end. **Amen.**

### For Officers and Leaders in the Church

O Lord our God, the founder and keeper of the church, we thank thee that thou hast called these leaders to share in the work of thy kingdom. Grant them sincerity, singleness of mind, and humility as they accept the responsibilities laid upon them. Guide them in this work for thy church. Prosper their labours and counsels.

To us all, O God, grant the gift of thy Holy Spirit, that in thy service we may find perfect freedom, and that our work here may enrich the world thou camest to save; through Jesus Christ our Lord. **Amen.**

*Then shall the minister say to the people,*

In token of your continual support of the work and witness of these *teachers and officers* will you rise?

In the name of the Lord Jesus Christ, the King and Head of the church, I install you as *teachers and officers*. The blessing of God Almighty, Father, Son and Holy Spirit, be with you all. **Amen.**

*Then shall the minister give the right hand of fellowship to those who have been installed.*

*The people shall be seated, those installed shall return to their places and the minister shall continue the service of public worship or the leader shall continue the meeting of the organization concerned.*

# 9. THE DEDICATION OF MEMORIALS AND GIFTS

AN ORDER FOR
**THE DEDICATION OF
MEMORIALS AND GIFTS**

*The service shall begin with the APPROACH and the WORD
OF GOD as in the First Order of Public Worship. It shall
then proceed as follows,*

**The Response**

*The offerings of the people shall be collected and presented.
An offertory prayer shall be said.*

*A hymn appropriate to the occasion shall be sung.*

*During the singing of the hymn the minister, accompanied
by any who are to take part with him in the service, shall
proceed to that part of the church where the act of dedication is to take place.*

*The people shall remain standing.*

*A prayer of invocation shall be said.*

Lord God almighty, by whose power, wisdom and
love all things are sanctified and made perfect, be
merciful to us and bless us. Cause thy face to shine
upon us, that what we now do in thy name may be
to thy glory; through Jesus Christ our Lord. **Amen.**

*The object to be dedicated may be unveiled.*

*Then the donor, or representative of the congregation or of
the organization responsible for the memorial or gift, shall
say,*

Sir, in memory of (*or* in the name of)  N. *Christian
names and surname*  we ask you to receive this memorial (*or* gift) and to dedicate it to the glory and
praise of God.

*The minister shall say,*

We accept this memorial (*or* gift) with gratitude,
and promise to use it in God's service.

We dedicate this memorial (*or* gift) to the glory and praise of God; in the name of the Father, and of the Son, and of the Holy Spirit. **Amen.**

*The people shall be seated.*

*Then shall be said prayers of appropriate thanksgiving, after which shall be said one of the following prayers.*

### Bible

Gracious God, who through the scriptures hast spoken thy word of judgement and mercy to each generation, let thy light and thy truth shine upon us from this Bible. Grant that, as we hear it read, we may enter into deeper knowledge of thy love in Jesus Christ our Lord. **Amen.**

### Pulpit

Almighty God, who hast given us thy word to be a lamp to our feet and a light to our path, grant that those who stand in this pulpit to preach may be guided by thy Holy Spirit, and that those who hear may be enabled by the same Spirit to receive thy word in faith and obedience. **Amen.**

### Communion Table

Lord Jesus Christ, who loved us and gave thyself for us, bless all who come to this thy Table. We pray that as they gather here thou mayest indeed be in their midst and that in communion with thee and with one another they may receive forgiveness of their sins and strength for thy service. **Amen.**

### Communion Vessels

Lord Jesus Christ, who in the upper room gave to the disciples the bread of life and the cup of the new covenant, constrain us by thy grace that, as we receive the bread and take the cup, our faith may be strengthened and our love increased.

**Amen.**

### Font

Almighty and ever-blessed God, who in thy great goodness hast given us a place within thy church and marked us with the seal of thy love in baptism, guide and uphold by thy Holy Spirit all who are baptized in this place. We pray that the children presented here may come to know and acknowledge thee, and that their parents may be faithful to their vows. We pray also for those who, confessing Jesus as Lord, are baptized here that they may be strengthened to bear witness of their love and loyalty to thee in the church and in the world.

**Amen.**

### Hymn Books

Almighty God, who hast bidden us to enter into thy gates with thanksgiving and into thy courts with praise, bless our use of these hymn books. Grant us thine aid that, singing psalms and hymns with heart and voice, we may also glorify thee with our lives until the day when we shall join in the perfected praise of all who have been redeemed by thy love. **Amen.**

### Organ or Other Musical Instrument

Almighty and ever-blessed God, to whom all praise belongs, accept the *organ* which we have dedicated to thy service. Grant that through its use worship in this house may be beautified with music and hearts may be lifted up to sing a new song to thee. And teach us, O Lord, to praise thee not only with our lips but in our lives that all that we have and are may glorify thee. **Amen.**

### Window

Almighty God, whose love shineth in all that thou hast made, accept the window we have dedicated to thee. Grant that we may ever worship thee in the beauty of holiness and care for the things that are true and good and lovely. **Amen.**

### Other Gifts

Almighty God, our heavenly Father, accept this gift for the enrichment of thy worship and the beauty of thy house. Grant to us the assurance that whatever is given or done in faith and love is, in thy sight, a gift to him who loved us and gave himself for us. **Amen.**

*Prayers of intercession shall follow.*

*The Lord's Prayer shall be said by minister and people.*

*A hymn shall be sung.*

*The minister shall dismiss the people with a blessing.*

# IV. TABLE OF LESSONS

## Introduction

The following table of lessons is offered as a means whereby over a three-year period the main themes of Scripture may be set before a congregation comprehensively and systematically. In the hope that it may also serve as a vehicle for teaching and preaching, an attempt has been made to secure coherence in the lessons for each service as well as continuity from Sunday to Sunday. The headings are intended to convey at a glance a major theme of each day's readings and to place the readings in a meaningful sequence, but they do not necessarily refer directly to each lesson.

The lectionary consists of three complete series of readings, each of which forms a unit in itself. They correspond roughly with the cycle of the New Curriculum and will be used most effectively in conjunction with it. In Year 1, God's Purpose, attention is concentrated upon the mighty acts of God. In Year 2, God's Way, aspects of Christian living predominate. Year 3, God's People, contains a fair amount of historical and biographical material. Examination of the headings for this year will disclose a story line that is first carried by the Old Testament passages, later taken up by the gospels, and then completed by a number of readings from Acts.

For reasons both of logic and of practicality, the structure does not correspond precisely with that of the traditional Christian Year. Its logical order, as suggested by Dr. A. A. McArthur, is that of the Apostles' Creed. The season of Creation, an innovation proposed by Dr. McArthur, marks the activities of God the Father and emphasizes his role in the natural order. The seasons taking their names from Christmas and Easter trace the career of the Son from the first anticipation of his coming to his exaltation and continual intercession for us. During Pentecost and the Sundays following it our attention is turned to the Holy Spirit, the church and the Christian hope.

Practical considerations have also been kept in mind. The year begins, as it effectively does in most congregations, on the Sunday after Labour Day. It reaches a climax in June, when most people are still worshipping in their home churches. Provision is made, so far as possible, for such commonly observed occasions as World-wide Communion Sunday and the Week of Prayer for Christian Unity.

Vagaries of the calendar make it impossible to use all the sets of lessons provided in any one year. It is suggested that readings for the Sundays after Christmas should be broken off in time to allow for the inclusion of all nine Sundays before Easter. When it is necessary to omit Sundays after Pentecost, this should be done early in the season so that the readings for the Seventh Sunday may be used on the second last Sunday in June and the series followed consecutively thereafter.

The number and nature of services held in the Christmas season and during Holy Week vary greatly from congregation to congregation. Readings are provided here for most possible occasions. Where such services are not customary, ministers may wish to use some of the readings provided for them on preceding Sundays. During Year 3, for the sake of those who are unable to attend Holy Week services, the entire Lenten series is built around persons associated with the passion.

Before the reading of the Gospel a selection from one of the Psalms is provided. The numbers refer to the selections found in the Service Book for the use of the people and not to the number of the Psalm as found in Scripture. An attempt has been made to secure coherence in the lessons and Psalm selection for each service.

This table is intended to be suggestive, not restrictive. When the calendar or local usage raise complications, or when circumstances suggest the use of other readings, the best criterion for selection will be the judgment of the minister.

| YEAR 1 | YEAR 2 | YEAR 3 |
|---|---|---|
| GOD'S PURPOSE | GOD'S WAY | GOD'S PEOPLE |

## The First Sunday in Creation

| *The creation of nature* | *The first-born of creation* | *The first people* |
|---|---|---|
| Gen. 1.1-25 | Prov. 8.22-31 | Gen. 3.1-13, 22-24 |
| Rev. 4 | Col. 1.15-20 | Rom. 5.12-21 |
| Psalm selection 10 | Psalm selection 1 | Psalm selection 71 |
| John 1.1-5 | John 1.1-14 | Mt. 18.7-14 |

## The Second Sunday in Creation

| *The creation of man* | *Man's dependence on God* | *Confusion of tongues* |
|---|---|---|
| Gen. 1.26-31 | Jer. 17.5-8 | Gen. 11.1-9 |
| I John 3.1-9 | Eph. 6.10-20 | II Cor. 4.1-6 |
| Psalm selection 1 | Psalm selection 16 | Psalm selection 45 |
| Luke 12.1-7 | Mt. 6.25-34 | Mark 13.14-27 |

## The Third Sunday in Creation

| *The creation of the family* | *Man's response to God* | *The promise to Abraham* |
|---|---|---|
| Gen. 2.18-25 | Isa. 55.6-13 | Gen. 12.1-9 |
| Eph. 5.25-6.4 | I Peter 1.13-21 | Gal. 3.1-14 |
| Psalm selection 14 | Psalm selection 3 | Psalm selection 78 |
| Mark 10.1-9 | Mt. 6.5-15 | John 8.54-59 |

## The Fourth Sunday in Creation

If there are not five Sundays in September, these lessons may be read on the Seventh Sunday in Creation.

| *The power of God* | *Man's life in God* | *God's new people* |
|---|---|---|
| Job 37.14-24 | II Chr. 1.7-12 | Deut. 30.1-14 |
| Rom. 9.14-26 | I Thess. 5.14-28 | Col. 1.3-14 |
| Psalm selection 68 | Psalm selection 84 | Psalm selection 1 |
| Mt. 14.22-33 | Mt. 7.1-12 | Luke 12.22-34 |

## The Fifth Sunday in Creation (World-wide Communion Sunday)

| *Provision for spiritual needs* | *Bread of life* | *The passover* |
|---|---|---|
| Isa. 55.1-5 | Exod. 16.1-8, 13-15 | Exod. 12.1-14 |
| I John 1.1-7 | I Cor. 11.23-28 | I Cor. 5.6-8 |
| Psalm selection 9 | Psalm selection 69 | Psalm selection 13 |
| Luke 10.38-11.4 | John 6.26-40 | John 6.48-63 |

## The Sixth Sunday in Creation (Sunday before Thanksgiving Day)

| *Provision for material needs* | *Thanksgiving* | *A good land* |
|---|---|---|
| Deut. 32.7-14; 33.26, 27a | Gen. 8.13-22 | Deut. 26.1-11 |
| Acts 14.8-18 | Col. 3.12-17 | II Cor. 9.6-15 |
| Psalm selection 67 | Psalm selection 7 | Psalm selection 66 |
| Mark 8.1-9 | Luke 17.11-19 | Luke 12.13-21 |

| YEAR 1 | YEAR 2 | YEAR 3 |
|--------|--------|--------|
| **GOD'S PURPOSE** | **GOD'S WAY** | **GOD'S PEOPLE** |

## The Seventh Sunday in Creation

| *The speaking God* | *Stewardship* | *The covenant* |
|---|---|---|
| Exod. 3.1-7 | Gen. 9.1-7 | Josh. 24.14-27 |
| Heb. 4.1-13 | I Peter 4.1-11 | Acts 3.22-26 |
| Psalm selection 80 | Psalm selection 18 | Psalm selection 40 |
| John 3.31-36 | Mt. 25.14-30 | John 15.18-27 |

## The Eighth Sunday in Creation

| *The hidden God* | *Obedience* | *A rebellious people* |
|---|---|---|
| Exod. 33.18-23 | Exod. 20.1-21 | I Sam. 8 |
| Rom. 11.33-36 | Phil. 4.8,9 | Rom. 7.5-13 |
| Psalm selection 49 | Psalm selection 74 | Psalm selection 43 |
| Luke 10.17-24 | Mark 12.28-34 | Mt. 11.16-24 |

## The Ninth Sunday in Creation (All Saints')

| *The holy God* | *Wholeness* | *The line of David* |
|---|---|---|
| Isa. 6.1-8 | Deut. 7.6-11 | I Sam. 16.1-13 |
| Rev. 15.1-4 | Rom. 1.1-7 | Acts 2.22-36 |
| Psalm selection 27 | Psalm selection 75 | Psalm selection 99 |
| John 8.12-20 | Mt. 5.38-48 | Mt. 22.41-45 |

## The Tenth Sunday in Creation (Remembrance Sunday)

| *The Lord of nations* | *Taking and giving life* | *Remembrance* |
|---|---|---|
| Isa. 40.12-26 | II Sam. 23.13-17 | II Sam. 1.17-27 |
| Eph. 1.15-23 | James 4.1-10 | Rev. 14.13-15.4 |
| Psalm selection 30 | Psalm selection 65 or 81 | Psalm selection 30 |
| Mark 12.13-17 | Mt. 10.34-39 | John 15.12-17 |

## The Eleventh Sunday in Creation

| *The protector of the humble* | *Wisdom* | *A house for the Lord* |
|---|---|---|
| Isa. 40.27-31 | Prov. 3.13-23 | I Kings 8.12-30 |
| Rev. 7.9-17 | James 3.13-18 | I Cor. 3.10-17 |
| Psalm selection 41 | Psalm selection 88 | Psalm selection 32 |
| Luke 18.1-8 | Luke 6.39-45 | Mt. 12.1-8 |

## The Twelfth Sunday in Creation

| *The spoiling of creation* | *Perils along the way* | *Judgment on God's people* |
|---|---|---|
| Gen. 6.5-22 | Num. 20.1-12 | II Kings 17.6-20 |
| Rom. 1.18-25 | James 3.1-12 | Rom. 2.1-11 |
| Psalm selection 46 | Psalm selection 15 | Psalm selection 34 |
| Mark 7.1-16 | Mt. 18.1-6 | Mark 12.1-12 |

## The Fourth Sunday Before Christmas

| *God's promise* | *Repentance* | *Exile and persecution* |
|---|---|---|
| Isa. 60.15-22 | Mal. 3.1-7b | Dan. 3 or 3.13-28 |
| Gal. 3.15-22 | Rev. 3.14-22 | Rev. 18.21-24 |
| Psalm selection 100 | Psalm selection 39 | Psalm selection 38 |
| Luke 1.5-25 | Luke 3.1-17 | Mt. 10.24-33 |

| YEAR 1 | YEAR 2 | YEAR 3 |
|---|---|---|
| **GOD'S PURPOSE** | **GOD'S WAY** | **GOD'S PEOPLE** |

## The Third Sunday Before Christmas

| *The word of promise* | *Vigilance* | *Return from exile* |
|---|---|---|
| Isa. 45.18-25 | Hab. 2.1-4 | Zech. 2.1-12 |
| Rom. 15.4-13 | Rom. 13.8-14 | Rom. 11.25-32 |
| Psalm selection 93 | Psalm selection 86 | Psalm selection 90 |
| Luke 1.26-38 | Mt. 25.1-13 | Luke 19.28-40 |

## The Second Sunday Before Christmas

| *The promise accepted* | *Hope* | *The forerunner* |
|---|---|---|
| I Sam. 2.1-10 | Lam. 3.19-33 | Isa. 62.10-12 |
| Heb. 11.1-3, 8-16 | Heb. 6.9-20 | Heb. 11.32-12.2 |
| Psalm selection 18 | Psalm selection 6 | Psalm selection 50 |
| Luke 1.39-56 | Luke 1.68-79 | John 1.19-28 |

## The First Sunday Before Christmas

| *Fulfilment draws near* | *Receiving Christ* | *News of a Saviour* |
|---|---|---|
| Isa. 40.1-11 | Isa. 35.1-10 | Jer. 23.5-8 |
| Phil. 4.4-7 | I Peter 1.22-2.3 | I John 4.13-21 |
| Psalm selection 24 | Psalm selection 2 | Psalm selection 2 |
| Luke 1.57-66 | Mark 9.33-37 | Mt. 1.18-25 |

## Christmas Eve

| *God with us* | *Peace on earth* | *The Christ Child* |
|---|---|---|
| Isa. 12 | Isa. 2.2-4 | Isa. 9.2-7 |
| Titus 3.3-7 | I John 2.7-11 | Titus 2.11-14 |
| Psalm selection 23 | Psalm selection 98 | Psalm selection 97 |
| Luke 2.1-20 | Luke 2.1-20 | Luke 2.1-20 |

## Christmas Day

| *The word made flesh* | *Good will to men* | *Wise men from the east* |
|---|---|---|
| Isa. 11.1-9 | Micah 5.2-5a | Isa. 60.1-14 |
| Heb. 1.1-12 | I John 4.7-12 | Gal. 4.1-7 |
| Psalm selection 73 | Psalm selection 8 | Psalm selection 11 |
| John 1.6-18 | John 3.16-21 | Mt. 2.1-12 |

## The First Sunday After Christmas

| *A sign to be spoken against* | *Brothers to Christ* | *Not many mighty* |
|---|---|---|
| Exod. 1.15-2.10 | I Sam. 1.19b-28 | Hosea 11.1-4, 8, 9 |
| II Tim. 1.3-14 | Heb. 2.9-18 | I Cor. 1.26-31 |
| Psalm selection 60 | Psalm selection 55 | Psalm selection 77 |
| Luke 2.22-35 | Luke 2.41-52 | Mt. 2.13-23 |

## New Year's Eve

| *Acceptable time* | *Foundations* | *A people prepared* |
|---|---|---|
| Eccl. 3.1-15 | Prov. 4.10-18 | Deut. 11.13-21 |
| II Cor. 6.1-10 | Heb. 12.25-29 | I Peter 3.8-16 |
| Psalm selection 42 | Psalm selection 5 | Psalm selection 75 |
| Luke 5.33-39 | Mt. 7.21-27 | Luke 12.35-48 |

| YEAR 1 | YEAR 2 | YEAR 3 |
|---|---|---|
| **GOD'S PURPOSE** | **GOD'S WAY** | **GOD'S PEOPLE** |

## The Second Sunday After Christmas (Epiphany)

| *Behold the Lamb of God* | *The healing of the nations* | *Good news to all nations* |
|---|---|---|
| Isa. 49.1-7 | Isa. 66.18-23 | Isa. 62.1-7 |
| Eph. 3.1-13 | Rev. 21.22-22.5 | Rom. 11.13-24 |
| Psalm selection 12 | Psalm selection 24 | Psalm selection 5 |
| John 1.29-34 | Mt. 3.13-17 | Mark 1.1-11 |

## The Third Sunday After Christmas

| *Temptation overcome* | *The Christian ethic* | *Messengers of God* |
|---|---|---|
| Exod. 17.1-7 | Deut. 11.26-32 | Ezek. 3.16-21 |
| Heb. 4.14-5.10 | I Cor. 13 | Acts 4.1-4, 13-21 |
| Psalm selection 83 | Psalm selection 91 | Psalm selection 27 |
| Mt. 4.1-11 | Mt. 5.1-12 | Mt. 4.12-25 |

## The Fourth Sunday After Christmas (Week of Prayer for Christian Unity)

| *A house divided* | *At peace with one another* | *That they may be one* |
|---|---|---|
| Ezek. 37.15-24a | Isa. 11.10-13 | Zech. 14. 5b-11 |
| Eph. 2.11-22 | I Cor. 3.1-9 | I Cor. 12.12-31a |
| Psalm selection 74 | Psalm selection 16 | Psalm selection 26 |
| Mt. 12.22-37 | Mark 9.38-50 | John 17.20-26 |

## The Fifth Sunday After Christmas

| *A miracle at Cana* | *Fulfilling the law* | *Not the righteous but sinners* |
|---|---|---|
| II Kings 4.1-7 | Deut. 10.12-22 | Isa. 43.18-21; 44.21-23 |
| I John 5.1-12 | I Tim. 1.1-11 | Acts 16.25-34 |
| Psalm selection 72 | Psalm selection 84 | Psalm selection 76 |
| John 2.1-11 | Mt. 5.17-20 | Mt. 9.9-17 |

## The Sixth Sunday After Christmas

| *Good news to the poor* | *By their fruits* | *Ministers of God* |
|---|---|---|
| Isa. 44.1-8 | Micah 6.1-8 | Exod. 18.13-27 |
| Acts 5.26-42 | James 1.16-27 | I Cor. 12.1-11 |
| Psalm selection 48 | Psalm selection 4 | Psalm selection 89 |
| Mt. 11.2-15 | Mt. 7.13-23 | Mark 3.7-19 |

## The Seventh Sunday After Christmas

| *Rejection at Nazareth* | *Fire on the earth* | *The family of Christ* |
|---|---|---|
| Isa. 61.1-9 | Jer. 23.23-32 | Amos 9.7-15 |
| Acts 4.5-12 | Rev. 8.1-5 | Rom. 8.12-17 |
| Psalm selection 36 | Psalm selection 40 | Psalm selection 17 |
| Luke 4.16-30 | Luke 12.49-59 | Mark 3.20-35 |

## The Eighth Sunday After Christmas

| *Lord of the Sabbath* | *Divine foolishness* | *Suffering saints* |
|---|---|---|
| Gen. 2.1-3 | Deut. 4.32-40 | Exod. 6.2-9 |
| Rom. 14.1-12 | I Cor. 3.18-23 | Rev. 12.7-12a |
| Psalm selection 25 | Psalm selection 79 | Psalm selection 36 |
| Mark 2.23-3.6 | Mark 10.13-16 | Mt. 14.1-12 |

| YEAR 1<br>**GOD'S PURPOSE** | YEAR 2<br>**GOD'S WAY** | YEAR 3<br>**GOD'S PEOPLE** |
|---|---|---|

## The Ninth Sunday Before Easter

| *The Messiah* | *One's hand to the plough* | *Upon this rock* |
|---|---|---|
| Isa. 42.1-9 | Josh. 1.1-9 | Exod. 19.1-8 |
| Rev. 1.4-8 | I Cor. 10.1-13 | I Peter 2.4-10 |
| Psalm selection 96 | Psalm selection 87 | Psalm selection 31 |
| Mark 8.27-38 | Luke 9.57-62 | Mt. 16.13-20 |

## The Eighth Sunday Before Easter

| *The transfigured Lord* | *Counting the cost* | *The transfiguration* |
|---|---|---|
| Exod. 24.12-18 | II Sam. 24.18-25 | Exod. 34.29-35 |
| II Peter 1.16-21 | Acts 4.32-5.11 | II Cor. 3.7-18 |
| Psalm selection 97 | Psalm selection 65 | Psalm selection 93 |
| Mark 9.2-13 | Luke 14.25-35 | Mt. 17.1-13 |

## The Seventh Sunday Before Easter

| *By what authority?* | *Denying oneself* | *Judgment in God's house* |
|---|---|---|
| Ezek. 3.4-11 | Prov. 3.1-12 | Jer. 2.1-13 |
| Acts 4.5-12 | Col. 1.24-29 | I Peter 4.12-19 |
| Psalm selection 52 | Psalm selection 51 | Psalm selection 6 |
| Mt. 21.23-32 | Mt. 16.21-28 | Mt. 20.17-28 |

## The Sixth Sunday Before Easter (First in Lent)

| *His face to Jerusalem* | *True fasting* | *Judas: crime and punishment* |
|---|---|---|
| Joel 2.12-19 | Isa. 58.1-9a | Lam. 3.55-66 |
| II Tim. 2.1-13 | II Cor. 7.2-13a | Rom. 7.14-25 |
| Psalm selection 47 | Psalm selection 85 | Psalm selection 46 |
| Luke 9.51-56 | Mt. 6.16-18 | John 13.16-30 |

## The Fifth Sunday Before Easter (Second in Lent)

| *Finding the sheep* | *True wealth* | *Peter: sin and redemption* |
|---|---|---|
| Jer. 31.10-14 | Eccl. 5.8-20 | II Sam. 12.1-13 |
| I Peter 2.18-25 | James 1.2-11 | Acts 3.11-21 |
| Psalm selection 99 | Psalm selection 82 | Psalm selection 9 |
| Luke 15.1-10 | Mark 10.17-31 | John 18.12-27 |

## The Fourth Sunday Before Easter (Third in Lent)

| *Restoring the prodigal* | *True greatness* | *Pilate: two cities* |
|---|---|---|
| Hos. 14 | Eccl. 9.11-18 | Isa. 60.12-14 |
| I John 1.8-2.6 | II Cor. 11.19-31 | Phil. 3.17-4.1 |
| Psalm selection 61 | Psalm selection 17 | Psalm selection 95 |
| Luke 15.11-32 | Mt. 23.1-12 | John 18.28-40 |

## The Third Sunday Before Easter (Fourth in Lent)

| *Overcoming the world* | *False religion* | *The crowd: sinning in ignorance* |
|---|---|---|
| Isa. 63.1-6 | Isa. 30.8-18 | Isa. 59.1-3, 9-20 |
| Rom. 8.18-27 | Rev. 3.1-6 | I Tim. 1.12-17 |
| Psalm selection 44 | Psalm selection 49 | Psalm selection 47 |
| John 16.25-33 | Mt. 23.13-28 | John 19.1-16 |

| YEAR 1 | YEAR 2 | YEAR 3 |
|--------|--------|--------|
| **GOD'S PURPOSE** | **GOD'S WAY** | **GOD'S PEOPLE** |

## The Second Sunday Before Easter (Passion Sunday) (Fifth in Lent)

|  |  | *The thieves: the possibility of repentance* |
|---|---|---|
| *One man for the people* | *A new commandment* |  |
| Lev. 16.1-10, 20-22 | Deut. 6.1-15 | Ezek. 18.1-4,21-32 |
| Heb. 9.11-15 | I John 3.11-24 | Gal. 2.15-21 |
| Psalm selection 95 | Psalm selection 77 | Psalm selection 43 |
| John 11.47-57 | John 13.31-35 | Luke 23.39-43 |

## The First Sunday Before Easter (Palm Sunday) (Sixth in Lent)

| *The triumphal entry* | *The triumphal entry* | *The King of the Jews* |
|---|---|---|
| II Sam. 6.12-19 | Zech. 9.9-12 | II Sam. 7.1-17 |
| Heb. 12.18-24 | Phil. 2.1-11 | Rev. 19.11-16 |
| Psalm selection 4 | Psalm selection 7 | Psalm selection 100 |
| Mark 11.1-10 | John 12.12-19 | John 19.17-22 |

## Monday in Holy Week

| *Cleansing the temple* | *Cleansing the temple* | *Losing and saving life* |
|---|---|---|
| Jer. 7.1-15 | Isa. 1.10-20 | Gen. 22.1-14 |
| Acts 7.44-53 | I Cor. 6.1-11 | Phil. 3.4b-16 |
| Psalm selection 29 | Psalm selection 63 | Psalm selection 79 |
| Luke 19.41-48 | Mark 11.15-18 | John 12.20-26 |

## Tuesday in Holy Week

| *The stone rejected* | *A house desolate* | *While we were yet sinners* |
|---|---|---|
| Isa. 5.1-7 | Zech. 7.8-8.8 | Isa. 50.4-9a |
| I Cor. 2.1-10 | Gal. 4.21-31 | Rom. 5.1-11 |
| Psalm selection 70 | Psalm selection 90 | Psalm selection 37 |
| Luke 20.9-19 | Mt. 23.29-24.2 | John 12.27-36a |

## Wednesday in Holy Week

| *The temple replaced* | *The aroma of Christ* | *Unbelief* |
|---|---|---|
| Jer. 22.1-9 | Isa. 43.1-7 | Deut. 31.24-29 |
| Heb. 9.23-28 | II Cor. 2.14-17 | Rom. 9.27-10.1 |
| Psalm selection 59 | Psalm selection 54 | Psalm selection 56 |
| Luke 21.5-19 | Mark 14.1-11 | John 12.36b-50 |

## Maundy Thursday

|  |  | *The sacrifice of praise and service* |
|---|---|---|
| *The covenant renewed* | *The last supper* |  |
| Exod. 12.21-28 | Jer. 31.31-34 | I Chr. 29.10-22a |
| Heb. 8.1-6 | Heb. 10.19-25 | Heb. 13.7-16 |
| Psalm selection 57 | Psalm selection 69 | Psalm selection 28 |
| Luke 22.7-23 | Mark 14.12-26 | John 13.1-15 |

## Good Friday

| *Christ crucified* | *The crucifixion* | *The crucifixion* |
|---|---|---|
| Exod. 14.8-14 | Isa. 53.7-12 | Isa. 52.13-53.6 |
| Col. 2.8-15 | Heb. 10.4-18 | I Peter 3.17-22 |
| Psalm selection 35 | Psalm selection 44 | Psalm selection 35 |
| Luke 22.63-23.49 | Mark 15.1-41 | John 19.23-42 |
| or 23.33-49 | or 15.6-15, 21-39 |  |

| YEAR 1 | YEAR 2 | YEAR 3 |
|---|---|---|
| **GOD'S PURPOSE** | **GOD'S WAY** | **GOD'S PEOPLE** |

## Easter Day

| | | |
|---|---|---|
| *The risen Lord* | *The resurrection* | *The resurrection* |
| Exod. 14.15-31 | Job 19.23-27b | Exod. 15.13-21 |
| Rev. 1.10-18 | I Cor. 15.1-11 | I Cor. 15.20-28 |
| Psalm selection 19 | Psalm selection 94 | Psalm selection 94 |
| Luke 23.50-24.12 | Mark 15.42-16.8 | John 20.1-10 |

## The First Sunday After Easter

| | | |
|---|---|---|
| *The Light of the world* | *Born anew* | *On the Emmaus road* |
| Num. 9.15-23 | Ezek. 11.14-20 | Zeph. 3.14-20 |
| Acts 26.1-20 | Rom. 6.3-14 | I Peter 1.3-12 |
| Psalm selection 89 | Psalm selection 64 | Psalm selection 26 |
| John 9.1-11 | John 3.1-15 | Luke 24.13-35 |

## The Second Sunday After Easter

| | | |
|---|---|---|
| *The good Shepherd* | *Sowing and reaping life* | *Chosen witnesses* |
| Ezek. 34.11-16 | I Kings 3.5-14 | Isa. 43.8-13 |
| Heb. 13.7-16, 20, 21 | Col. 3.1-11 | Acts 10.34-43 |
| Psalm selection 53 | Psalm selection 62 | Psalm selection 61 |
| John 10.1-18 | John 4.31-38 | John 20.19-31 |

## The Third Sunday After Easter

| | | |
|---|---|---|
| *The Resurrection and the Life* | *The Son gives life* | *Communion with the risen Christ* |
| Job 33.14-18, 23-28 | Isa. 25.1-9 | Isa. 63.7-14 |
| I Cor. 15.51-58 | II Cor. 4.7-18 | Acts 13.16a, 26-33 |
| Psalm selection 25 | Psalm selection 59 | Psalm selection 73 |
| John 11.17-44 | John 5.19-29 | John 21.1-14 |

## The Fourth Sunday After Easter

| | | |
|---|---|---|
| *The true Vine* | *Caring for the flock* | *The commission to Peter* |
| S. of S. 2.8-17 | Ezek. 34.25-31 | Jer. 23.1-4 |
| Rom. 8.1-11 | Acts 20.28-35 | I Peter 5.1-11 |
| Psalm selection 50 | Psalm selection 53 | Psalm selection 53 |
| John 15.1-11 | John 10.22-29 | John 21.15-19 |

## The Fifth Sunday After Easter (Sunday before Ascension)

| | | |
|---|---|---|
| *The ascended Lord* | *Preparing a place* | *The ascension* |
| Exod. 19.16-20 | II Kings 2.1-15 | Deut. 34.1-8 |
| Rev. 5.6-14 | Eph. 4.1-16 | Acts 1.1-11 |
| Psalm selection 21 | Psalm selection 12 | Psalm selection 21 |
| Luke 24.44-53 | John 14.1-14 | John 16.1-15 |

## The Sixth Sunday After Easter (Sunday after Ascension)

| | | |
|---|---|---|
| *The glorified Christ* | *The interceding Christ* | *Awaiting the Spirit* |
| Dan. 7.9-14 | Gen. 28.10-22 | Isa. 32.9-18 |
| II Cor. 5.14-21 | Rom. 8.33-39 | Acts 1.12-26 |
| Psalm selection 96 | Psalm selection 24 | Psalm selection 54 |
| John 17.1-11a | John 17.11b-19 | John 16.16-24 |

| YEAR 1 | YEAR 2 | YEAR 3 |
|---|---|---|
| **GOD'S PURPOSE** | **GOD'S WAY** | **GOD'S PEOPLE** |

## Pentecost

| | | |
|---|---|---|
| *The new Teacher* | *The gift of the Spirit* | *The Spirit bestowed* |
| Deut. 5.1-21 | Joel 2.23-32a | Ezek. 36.22-28 |
| Acts 2.1-13 | Acts 2.1-13 | Acts 2.1-21 |
| Psalm selection 76 | Psalm selection 10 | Psalm selection 62 |
| John 14.15-31a | Luke 11.5-13 | John 7.37-44 |

## The First Sunday After Pentecost

| | | |
|---|---|---|
| *Telling good news* | *A choice of ways* | *The community of the Spirit* |
| Isa. 52.7-10 | Deut. 30.15-20 | Num. 11.24-29 |
| I Cor. 9.13-18 | Gal. 5.16-26 | Acts 2.37-47 |
| Psalm selection 92 | Psalm selection 74 | Psalm selection 14 |
| Luke 10.1-16 | Mark 4.1-20 | Luke 12.8-12 |

## The Second Sunday After Pentecost

| | | |
|---|---|---|
| *God and the sinner* | *Turning to God* | *The conversion of Paul* |
| Micah 7.18-20 | Isa. 54.1-8 | Jer. 1.4-10 |
| Gal. 6.1-10 | Rom. 6.15-23 | Acts 9.1-19a |
| Psalm selection 58 | Psalm selection 68 | Psalm selection 48 |
| John 7.53-8.11 | Luke 19.1-10 | Mt. 9.35-10.1 |

## The Third Sunday After Pentecost

| | | |
|---|---|---|
| *God's invitation* | *Life's ultimates* | *The baptism of Cornelius* |
| Hosea 2.16-23 | Gen. 32.22-32 | Zech. 8.18-23 |
| I Cor. 1.18-25 | Eph. 3.14-21 | Acts 11.1-18 |
| Psalm selection 33 | Psalm selection 28 | Psalm selection 8 |
| Luke 14.15-24 | Mt. 13.44-52 | Mark 7.24-30 |

## The Fourth Sunday After Pentecost

| | | |
|---|---|---|
| *Neither Jew nor Greek* | *The perils of affluence* | *A call to Macedonia* |
| Ruth 1.8-18 | Exod. 32.1-4 | Jonah 3 |
| Gal. 3.23-29 | I Tim. 6.6-19 | Acts 16.6-15 |
| Psalm selection 85 | Psalm selection 83 | Psalm selection 63 |
| John 4.1-26 | Luke 16.1-13 | Mt. 28.16-20 |

## The Fifth Sunday After Pentecost

| | | |
|---|---|---|
| *The coming kingdom* | *Power in weakness* | *Paul at Athens* |
| Joel 2.1-11 | Zech. 4.1-10 | Job 28.12-28 |
| I Thess. 5.1-11 | II Cor. 12.1-10 | Acts 17.16-34 |
| Psalm selection 20 | Psalm selection 82 | Psalm selection 16 |
| Mark 4.21-34 | Luke 17.5-10 | John 8.31-38 |

## The Sixth Sunday After Pentecost

| | | |
|---|---|---|
| *The day of the Lord* | *Enduring to the end* | *Paul at Rome* |
| Zeph. 1.14-18 | Amos 5.18-24 | Jonah 3.10-4.11 |
| II Peter 3.9-13 | Rev. 2.8-11 | Acts 28.11-31 |
| Psalm selection 13 | Psalm selection 22 | Psalm selection 57 |
| Luke 17.20-37 | Mark 13.1-13 | Mark 16.15-20 |
| | | *or* John 4.39-42 |

| YEAR 1 | YEAR 2 | YEAR 3 |
|---|---|---|
| **GOD'S PURPOSE** | **GOD'S WAY** | **GOD'S PEOPLE** |

## The Seventh Sunday After Pentecost (Second last in June)

| *The fulness of time* | *Final judgment* | *A new heaven and a new earth* |
|---|---|---|
| Isa. 64.1-9 | Micah 4.1-4 | Isa. 65.17-25 |
| Eph. 1.3-14 | Rev. 19.1-10 | Rev. 21.1-7 |
| Psalm selection 97 | Psalm selection 42 | Psalm selection 20 |
| Mark 13.28-37 | Mt. 25.31-46 | Luke 13.22-30 |

## The Eighth Sunday After Pentecost (Sunday before Dominion Day)

| *God and Caesar* | *Treasure in heaven* | *A remade society* |
|---|---|---|
| Deut. 8 | Prov. 8.1-21 | Isa. 32.1-4, 16-18 |
| Rom. 13.1-7 | I Peter 2.11-17 | Rev. 11.15-19 |
| Psalm selection 81 | Psalm selection 31 | Psalm selection 98 |
| Mt. 22.15-20 | Mt. 6.19-24 | Luke 22.24-30 |

## The Ninth Sunday After Pentecost

| *The hungry fed* | *True religion* | *From faith to faith* |
|---|---|---|
| I Kings 17.8-16 | Lev. 19.9-18 | Isa. 45.1-8 |
| Acts 6.1-7 | Rom. 12.9-21 | Rom. 1.8-17 |
| Psalm selection 66 | Psalm selection 80 | Psalm selection 60 |
| Mark 6.30-44 | Luke 6.32-38 | Mt. 8.1-13 |

## The Tenth Sunday After Pentecost

| *Evil forces expelled* | *Law and freedom* | *The justified community* |
|---|---|---|
| Isa. 29.13-24 | Exod. 31.12-17 | Exod. 12.51-13.10 |
| Acts 8.4-13 | Gal. 5.1-15 | Rom. 3.21-30 |
| Psalm selection 86 | Psalm selection 3 | Psalm selection 45 |
| Mark 1.21-28 | Mt. 12.9-14 | Luke 18.9-14 |

## The Eleventh Sunday After Pentecost

| *The sick healed* | *Humility* | *Christ in the midst* |
|---|---|---|
| Ezek. 47.1-12 | Isa. 57.14-19 | Exod. 40.17-38 |
| Acts 3.1-10 | James 2.1-12 | Phil. 1.3-11 |
| Psalm selection 64 | Psalm selection 41 | Psalm selection 52 |
| Mark 1.29-39 | Luke 14.1-11 | Mt. 18.15-20 |

## The Twelfth Sunday After Pentecost

| *The deaf made to hear* | *Self-examination* | *Salt of the earth* |
|---|---|---|
| Isa. 42.18-43.7 | Prov. 16.1-9 | Isa. 4.2-6 |
| Rom. 10.5-17 | I Cor. 9.19-27 | Phil. 2.12-18 |
| Psalm selection 87 | Psalm selection 39 | Psalm selection 78 |
| Mark 7.31-37 | Mt. 5.27-37 | Mt. 5.13-16 |

## The Thirteenth Sunday After Pentecost

| *The blind made to see* | *Justice* | *Hated for his sake* |
|---|---|---|
| Isa. 42.14-16 | Amos 5.1-15 | Dan. 6.1-23 |
| Acts 21.39-22.16 | James 5.1-12 | Acts 6.8-10; 7.54-60 |
| Psalm selection 92 | Psalm selection 51 | Psalm selection 38 |
| Mark 10.46-52 | Luke 16.19-31 | Mt. 10.16-23 |

| YEAR 1<br>**GOD'S PURPOSE** | YEAR 2<br>**GOD'S WAY** | YEAR 3<br>**GOD'S PEOPLE** |
|---|---|---|

## The Fourteenth Sunday After Pentecost

| *The infirm made whole* | *Forgiveness* | *The responsible community* |
|---|---|---|
| II Kings 5.1-14 | Gen. 50.15-21 | Deut. 4.5-14 |
| James 5.13-20 | Eph. 4.25-5.2 | Eph. 5.15-21 |
| Psalm selection 56 | Psalm selection 37 | Psalm selection 33 |
| Mark 2.1-12 | Mt. 18.21-35 | Luke 19.11-27 |

## The Fifteenth Sunday After Pentecost

| *Spirits renewed* | *Brotherhood* | *The sharing community* |
|---|---|---|
| Isa. 30.19-26 | Gen. 4.1-15 | Job 31.13-22 |
| Eph. 4.17-24 | Rom. 14.13-15.2 | I Cor. 16.1-9 |
| Psalm selection 34 | Psalm selection 75 | Psalm selection 32 |
| Mark 5.1-20 | Mt. 5.21-26 | Mark 12.38-44 |

## The Sixteenth Sunday After Pentecost

| *The dead brought to life* | *Service* | *The witnessing community* |
|---|---|---|
| Ezek. 37.1-14 | Exod. 23.6-12 | Ezek. 33.1-9 |
| I Cor. 15.35-50 | James 2.14-25 | Col. 4.2-6 |
| Psalm selection 68 | Psalm selection 84 | Psalm selection 23 |
| Mt. 9.18-26 | Luke 10.25-37 | John 1.35-51 |

## The Seventeenth Sunday After Pentecost

| *The storm stilled* | *Generosity* | *A community on trial* |
|---|---|---|
| I Kings 19.1-15a | I Chr. 29.1-9 | Jer. 18.1-11 |
| Acts 27.27-44 | II Cor. 8.1-9 | II Peter 1.1-11 |
| Psalm selection 22 | Psalm selection 72 | Psalm selection 29 |
| Mark 4.35-41 | Mt. 6.1-4 | Mt. 13.24-30 |

## The Last Sunday After Pentecost (Labour Sunday)

| *God at work* | *Labour and rest* | *God's workers* |
|---|---|---|
| Isa. 45.9-13 | Neh. 6.1-9 | Exod. 35.30-36.1 |
| Rom. 8.28-32 | II Thess. 3.6-13 | Eph. 2.1-10 |
| Psalm selection 11 | Psalm selection 91 | Psalm selection 88 |
| John 5.1-18 | Mt. 11.25-30 | Mt. 20.1-16 |

## DATE DUE

| | | | |
|---|---|---|---|
| | | | |
| | | | |
| | | | |
| | | | |
| | | | |
| | | | |
| | | | |
| | | | |
| | | | |
| | | | |
| | | | |
| | | | |
| | | | |
| | | | |
| | | | |
| | | | |
| | | | |
| | | | |
| | | | |
| | | | Printed in USA |

# The Nicene Creed

*Minister.*

Let us repeat together the historic expression of Christian faith known as the Nicene Creed.

*Minister and People.*

We believe in one God, the Father almighty,
    maker of heaven and earth,
    and of all things visible and invisible:
And in one Lord Jesus Christ,
    the only-begotten Son of God,
    begotten of his Father before all worlds,
    God of God, light of light,
    very God of very God
    begotten not made,
    being of one substance with the Father,
    by whom all things were made:
Who for us men, and for our salvation,
    came down from heaven,
    and was incarnate by the Holy Spirit of the Virgin Mary,
    and was made man,
    and was crucified for us under Pontius Pilate.
He suffered and was buried,
    and the third day he rose again according to the scriptures,
    and ascended into heaven,
    and sitteth on the right hand of the Father.
And he shall come again with glory
    to judge both the quick and the dead:
Whose kingdom shall have no end.

And we believe in the Holy Spirit,
    the Lord and giver of life,
    who proceedeth from the Father and the Son,
    who with the Father and Son together
        is worshipped and glorified,
    who spake by the prophets.

And we believe in one holy catholic and apostolic church.
We acknowledge one baptism for the remission of sins.
And we look for the resurrection of the dead,
    and the life of the world to come. *Amen.*